The Player's Journal

A 30-day program of basketball skills training for players who want to take ownership of their development.

© 2020 Published by Factory Sports, Inc.
17543 Nassau Commons Blvd.
Lewes, DE 19958
www.FactorySportsDE.com

All Scripture quotations are taken from the *New King James Version*. Copyright 1982 by Thomas Nelson. Used by permission. All rights reserved.

Dedication

I would like to dedicate this work to:

<u>My Wife, Brandi</u>
I often wonder if I would accomplish anything without you. You motivate me, inspire me, challenge me and encourage me. You are my coach.

<u>My Players</u>
I am constantly learning from you. You push the boundaries of your abilities and try to find new ways to improve. Thank you for being coachable. Thank you for trusting me to be a part of your development.

<u>My 2019-2020 Cape Henlopen Basketball Team</u>
...and all other basketball players that had their season cancelled during the 2020 COVID-19 pandemic. You may have had a dream dissolved. You may have had growth, progress and opportunity hindered for a time. And though you spent months quarantined without coaches or teammates or competition, you still sought ways to improve on your own. You bounced back as always. This book is for you.

Coach Woods With The Assist!
by Art Perry, Spring 2020

The coronavirus pandemic has created a new reality in the approach to sports! How we watch, play and train is affected by this disease. We must incorporate safety procedures in our daily lives to avoid the virus. Athletic development in individual and team sports must adjust to this new environment. We must find ways to maintain our development and reach the ultimate goals we set.

The Player's Journal is an "assist" to athletes who seek excellence! It is designed to help you improve and grow through a mentality of maturation and developing discipline, accountability and desire needed to be the best you can be!

Coach Art Perry (center) has plenty of experience as he coached for Rutgers University during their historic Final Four appearance in 1976 as well as assisting at UConn, American University, Delaware State University, University of Maryland and the Washington Wizards. Coach Perry and Coach Woods became friends after Coach Perry retired to Delaware.

Your Basketball Journey

by Jerry Peden, Sr. Spring 2020

You are about to embark on an exciting journey in the game of basketball. The road to success has not drastically changed in recent times. Players like you must take ownership of your own development. Coach Pat Woods has developed *The Player's Journal* with you in mind as a road map for your development. This idea for *The Player's Journal* developed from a basketball camp notebook that I gave campers back when he was in 7th grade. Coach Woods used the ideas in the notebook and developed into a very good basketball player himself. Now, you are fortunate to have the same opportunity to be as good as you want to be by using *The Player's Journal* to develop into a GREAT player. Basketball is a game of HABITS, which must be developed and practiced over and over through the process of repetition. This journal will provide you with the drills and best techniques to make you better each and every day. Your progression to becoming a GREAT player, then, is dependent on your willingness to put in time. Your determination to put in the time and effort to work on the developmental skills outlined in *The Player's Journal* will determine how GREAT you will become.

Best of luck in one of the most exciting journeys of your life,

Coach Peden

Coach Jerry Peden, Sr. is one of the most winningest coaches in Delaware High School basketball. Though he only coached Woods for one year in high school, the two have stayed in contact ever since.

Table of Contents

There comes a time in every player's career when they must take responsibility for their growth as a player.

Everyday you will work on improving your defense, dribble attack, finishing around the rim, shooting, and offensive footwork

Everyday you will be asked questions designed to remind you about your overall purpose in training. Each day you will asked to evaluate yourself. You will also hold yourself accountable to those other duties that make a player someone that every coach wants.

Here you will find an explanation about the practice plan and the response page as well as some other suggestions to help with your daily routine.

Days 1-10. Getting started and getting to work.

Days 11-20. Gaining momentum and pressing on.

Days 21-30. Finish strong.

This is where you record your scores and times from the drills. You will record your first attempt as well as your personal best. Look here for your objective proof that you improved over the course of your training.

Basketball is a competitive game and in order to reach your potential your training must continue in competition and strength and conditioning. Remember to be smart in your training. Now go write your story!

Diagrams, pictures, and instructions for every drill in this journal.

It's the small things that you do

when no one is watching

that enable you to do the great things

when everyone is watching.

Dear Player,

This journal is for you. It is a guide and encouragement to help you take ownership of your development as a basketball player and as a person.

I know who you are because many years ago I was you. And as a coach now, I see you in all my players. I know that once the season is over, many coaches are limited in their ability to help you develop over the next six to seven months. I also know that you may be limited in your ability to find a ride to the park or people to play with or a trainer to guide you. I know that fire within you that desires to improve knowing that your opponents may have more opportunities than you do. I also know that you will do whatever it takes to make sure you become the best basketball player possible, that you will let nothing stand in your way. And with all of that in mind, I have made this journal for you.

You see, when I was growing up I always wanted to play. Always. I would miss meals, lose sleep and skip parties just to play. But not everyone shared my desire. I was always looking for people to play with or open courts to play on. And in middle school I was always trying to find a ride to those places.

I spent most of my summer alone at home while my parents and older siblings were at work. I had a few friends in the neighborhood and spent time riding my bike to their houses and to the courts and we played as often as possible. I had no trainer, no coach, no program to follow. I only had a desire to play basketball and become the best I can be...and then my parents signed me up for basketball camp.

Camp was one week long and involved fundamental skill development, games and competitions ranging from one on one to five on five. Each day we had to memorize a quote and recite it as a group during breaks. During lunch we watched "The Pistol", a movie about the relentless drive and work ethic of a young Pete Maravich (NCAA All-Time Leading Scorer). All afternoon we played. I ate it up. I loved the competition.

After the camp was finished we were all given a basketball notebook. This notebook was a difference maker for me. I don't know how much the other guys used it but it became a teammate and a coach for me for the rest of the summer and summers to follow. It taught me how to effectively practice alone and I began to own my development as a player and as a person. I continued to own my development in my high school and college playing days and learned how to help my teammates take ownership of their development as well.

You see, dear friend, there is a skill in knowing WHY you need to train, WHAT skills you need to train and HOW you need to train. Once I was able to answer those three things, I was able to own my development and assist others in owning theirs. That time alone in the summer started my journey and has enabled me to help others start theirs. I continue to update, adjust and add to my coaching curriculum to this day. I have used this holistic training program with my players and teams from middle school through all levels of college basketball. I have also built my business, Factory Sports Inc. as a central hub for player development, a place "where players are made."

May this journal give you as much guidance, instruction and encouragement as I found in my basketball notebook. Thank you for allowing me to be a part of your journey to owning your development as a player and as a person. Let's get to work!

- Coach Woods

Own Your Development

I tell my players all the time, "Own your environment." Wherever you are and whatever is going on, YOU be in charge. When you flash to the high post, own that spot. Don't let anyone push you out of it. When there is a 50-50 ball, take charge and snatch it. If there is going to be peer pressure, you supply it. Whatever environment you are in, own it! Do the right thing and be a catalyst for others.

The same thing applies for your training. Practice isn't something done to you; it is something you do. Likewise, working out is something you do, not something done to you. YOU are the player. YOU will celebrate the wins and grieve the losses. YOU are the one who sweats and bleeds and cries. YOU are the one who is sore and tired. YOU have to push through the mental and physical fatigue. As a player YOU have to own all of these things. And here is the reason why:

When the smoke clears and the dust settles on your career, your success will come down to how much you maximized your talent through hard work and deliberate practice.

Those who passively allow life to happen to them rarely win. Take control of your development. If coaches and teammates and trainers can help you, then by all means invite them to join in but you must take responsibility for your development. You must be able to say that you did everything you could to go as far as you could.

No Excuses

There will be times throughout this program that you simply do not feel like working out. There will be times that you are sore, times when it is raining outside, times when you have a headache or something worse. But there will also be game days when you feel that way. There will always be times in life when you are faced with adversity but you have to get the job done anyway. You must prepare yourself for those times right now by learning to overcome obstacles.

"All adversity either becomes an obstacle you overcome or an excuse for why you failed."

The 2008 USA Olympic Basketball Team identified and recorded their "Gold Standards." This was a way for them to take ownership of their team and to be accountable to one another. They knew that if they would hold each other to these standards they would achieve their goal of Olympic Gold – the best team in the world. The first standard was this:

"No Excuses. We have what is takes to win."

Those who make excuses or place blame on someone or something else, do so to explain why they didn't achieve their goals. They point out reasons why they fell short. As a competitor you will be tempted to make excuses also. You must wage war against that temptation and overcome.

Own your environment! Be in charge of what is happening in your life. Don't be swayed by trends or circumstance or peer pressure. You BE the peer pressure.

So how about now? What will you do with today? Will you let it happen to you or will you make something happen? Will you own your development?

Team USA Gold Standards

- <u>No Excuses</u>: We have what it takes to win.
- <u>Great Defense</u>: This is the key to winning the gold. We do the dirty work.
- <u>Communication</u>: We look each other in the eye. We tell each other the truth.
- <u>Trust</u>: We believe in each other.
- <u>Collective Responsibility</u>: We are committed to each other. We win together.
- <u>Care</u>: We have each other's backs. We give aid to a teammate.
- <u>Respect</u>: We respect each other and our opponents. We're always on time. We're always prepared.
- <u>Intelligence</u>: We take good shots. We're aware of team fouls. We know the scouting report.
- <u>Poise</u>: We show no weakness.
- <u>Flexibility</u>: We can handle any situation. We don't complain.
- <u>Unselfishness</u>: We're connected. We make the extra pass. Our value is not measured in playing time.
- <u>Aggressiveness</u>: We play hard every possession.
- <u>Enthusiasm</u>: This is fun.
- <u>Performance</u>: We're hungry. We have no bad practices.
- <u>Pride</u>: We are the best team in the world and we represent the best country.

Mike Krzyzewski, "The Gold Standard: Building a World-Class Team"

My Story - Finding a Way

Back in seventh grade I didn't have all of the opportunities that players have today but I had the ability and assertiveness to own my development. One day after school, as I was walking to the bus, I noticed that the gym was completely empty. Now, to a basketball player, an empty gym is just too inviting to pass up. I knew I had to find a way to get in there.

I didn't have a ball. I didn't have permission. I would be missing the bus. I would be alone. These were all the excuses I had. They would either be the reasons why I didn't pursue this opportunity. OR...they would simply be the obstacles that I had to overcome to make it happen. I knew I had to find a way. A few small hurdles wouldn't stop me.

The next day, I told my parents I would need a ride home from school after their work day was complete. I packed my basketball in my backpack. I made a deal with custodian: I would mop the gym floor if he would let me play on it afterwards. Deal! I got my ball, I got my permission and I got my ride. All that was left was to figure out what to do while I was alone in the gym with my ball (which is exactly why I have created this journal). Development owned!

Years later, as a high school player, my coach would meet me in the gym before school (6:30am). I would wake up early, stop by Wawa for a breakfast sandwich and head to the gym. I would shoot as long as possible, take a shower and head to class.

At night, again, I would make a deal with the custodians of the school to mop the floor if I could use the gym. Many of the custodians were local basketball legends in their own right and would rebound for me or give me pointers. This was an unexpected reward of owning my development.

Owning your development has to do with the desire and determination to make sure you are doing what is necessary to give yourself a chance at being successful. It requires mental toughness and a refusal to be stopped by obstacles. It says, "nothing will prevent me from getting better."

What is Development?

Simply stated, development is about getting better. It involves **improving the skills you currently possess** so that they become "automatic." In other words, you can execute the skill with great speed and precision in small spaces and under pressure–without thinking about it.

The second component of development involves **adding skills that you currently don't possess.** These new skills will complement current skills. On the basketball court, this often looks like counter moves for when the defense hones in on your strengths. For example, if you have a really effective crossover, the defense will start anticipating it and moving to steal the ball from you. Now you can add a hesitation dribble as a set-up or fake the crossover with an in-and-out dribble.

Skill development requires you to name your strengths and weaknesses. You do not need to be able to do every move. You need to identify your strengths and master them.

"Be great at the things that you are good at."

Your weaknesses are those things that will beat you as a player. Think about how YOU would beat you. Then you can go to work to eliminate those things that are opportunities for your opponents. For example, if full court pressure defense will beat you and your team, then you must work to eliminate that weakness. This could involve greater conditioning, dribbling ability, poise under pressure, comfort handling the ball and understanding passing angles. Whatever the case may be, get to work eliminating any weakness in your game.

Commitment

A flash in the pan never gets it done. Development takes time. It takes consistency. It is about showing up and giving all you've got day in and day out. Be committed to the work and let the results take care of themselves. When things get tough, don't waver. When you face disappointment or discouragement, pick yourself up, dust yourself off and get back to work. Your commitment to the work is what will give you confidence for the performance.

Certainly you've seen the teams that get super hyped up right before the game. I did that as a player. I liked getting my nervous energy out. But when the ball is tossed up, none of the hype means anything. It is the team that put in the work when no one was watching that is ready.

It is the team that competes every possession with resilience and focus that imposes their will. It is the team that quickly bounces back from adversity with determination and confidence–not panicking and not turning from their course–that gets the job done. THAT is toughness! And that is what wins in games and in life.

DEFEAT

No one is beat 'til he quits

No one is through 'til he stops

No matter how often he drops

A fellow is not down 'til he lies

In the dust and refuses to rise

Fate can slam him and bang him
around

And batter his frame 'til he's sore

But he never can say that he's downed

While he bobs up serenely for more

A fellow's not down 'til he dies

Nor beat 'til no longer he tries.

Edgar Albert Guest

The Practice Plan

This chapter will explain the components of the daily practice plan and their importance. This will give you a better understanding of WHY you are doing WHAT you are doing.

Drills are designed to break down the game into small chunks so you can focus on acquiring the skills necessary to be successful in basketball. They help you improve in small parts of the game in order to produce growth in overall performance. These drills will not ask you to copy a specific eight-part move that might happen once in a season. That is more choreography than anything else. Instead these drills will teach you the eight parts, and then it is up to you to put them together in live play using your creativity and what is required by the play.

Skill development should progress through three stages: 1) acquiring the motor skills and coordination to perform the move, 2) adding necessary strength and speed (explosiveness) to do it quickly and powerfully, and 3) basketball IQ to know when to use the move in competition. In this journal we will be focusing on the first stage. Stage two is the reason that Factory Sports includes strength and conditioning in our player development programs. Stage three, basketball IQ, is trained in group practices and live competition.

At our gym, advanced high school and college players meet early each morning for speed and strength work followed individual skill development and deliberate practice in decision-making situations. We end every session with live competition playing anything from one on one to five on five, even adding limits to game play (such as every possession must include at least one ball screen or post entry).

In this journal the areas of focus are broken down for each day to ensure that you are developing all areas of your individual skills.

Take Your Vitamins

There are certain things that you must be doing everyday—like taking your vitamins! They are the easiest things to improve and those who excel at them become great players. These "vitamins" include ball handling, dribbling and shooting as well as a dynamic warm-up. If you are going to take your development seriously, you must prepare your body for the work. DO NOT NEGLECT WARMING UP! Or as coaches state it:

"Don't Get Bored with Getting Better"

Defense

Defense is one of the most neglected parts of individual skill development programs. Very few people work on their defense when training alone. Your diligence can give you the advantage here and allow you to separate yourself from the average player.

Anyone can be a great defender. First, it requires effort: maximum effort and multiple efforts. Where there is effort, there can be excellence. Someone willing to be relentless on the defensive end only needs to learn a few critical skills to be a good defender. The great defender then adds quick, precise footwork and an understanding of angles and timing. This journal provides the drills you will need to help you with the footwork and quickness. The effort is up to you!

Dribble Attack

There are two parts to that heading: Dribble and Attack. Dribbling for the sake of dribbling is a waste of everyone's time, particularly in a game. Few things in basketball are worse than the teammate's dribbling that goes nowhere. If you are going to dribble use it to attack and create.

This is the focus of these drills. You will first learn a variety of dribbling moves, and then you will practice putting them together in the combinations necessary to elude a defender and get to your desired spot on the court. You will practice attacking! You must keep that in the front of your mind while training. When you are thinking "attack," you will force yourself to be quick and precise with every movement. Putting pressure on the defense will create scoring opportunities for you and your teammates.

Finishing

In your finishing drills, you will work on scoring the ball in the interior. You will be utilizing your dribble attack and your footwork to get to the rim. Once you get there you must be able to finish. These drills will teach you to score from all angles, with either hand and with a variety of footwork.

Shooting

Shooting is perhaps the single most important skill in the game. It is very rare to find great basketball players who do not shoot well. And usually they are the very best at some other aspect of the game (Dikembe Mutombo at shot blocking, Dennis Rodman at rebounding, Rajon Rondo at passing, for example).

Shooting is technique and repetition. First you must understand and develop good shooting form. NBA shooting coach Dave Love teaches his players to focus on balance and hand placement (Jim Huber Podcast, November 2016). The drills in this journal will help you work on both of those aspects of shooting. From form shooting from a standing position to shooting off the dribble to shooting on the move, you will be able to concentrate on both your balance and the release of the basketball.

You must pay attention to consistencies in your shooting. Are you missing long? Short? Left? Right? Make necessary adjustments. Own your development! The shooting drills will ask you to record your scores and compete against a clock. This is to add pressure to your training and to measure your growth. Any time you can have someone rebound for you is a bonus. (It is also a requirement for the Loaded Cannon and Weber State License to Shoot drills.) Make sure you show your gratitude to your rebounders for assisting you in your development.

Footwork

Learn to love footwork. Precise footwork equals quickness and balance. Once you understand the proper footwork you can add speed to the steps of a drill. Concentrate on your balance and ability to be explosive off of each step. Also be ready to attack when your defender gets off balance. If you want to see great footwork, watch clips of Michael Jordan, Kobe Bryant, Hakeem Olajuwon and James Harden. Aside from all the other incredible things these players can do with a ball, their footwork always gave them great separation for their shots.

The Drills Index

In the back of this journal you will find The Drills Index, which includes detailed descriptions and instructions for each assigned drill. In addition to the instructions and pictures contained in this journal, all of the drills are demonstrated and explained on video at FactorySportsDE.com

"It is critical that players assume responsibility for improving through their effort and execution in practice sessions"

QUALITY ATTITUDE

The Mediocre Attitude

- Effort in practice fluctuates depending on their mood, whether they like the activity, or on external motivation.
- Practice is something "coach does to me"
- Players "go through the motions", "put in their time" and just want to finish the drills and get out of the practice.

The Professional Attitude

- Practice is viewed as an opportunity to improve and refine skills.
- Players ask themselves these questions: How can I get better? What am I going to accomplish today?
- Players set standards of performance and goals to be accomplished in practice.
- They evaluate their practice in terms of effort, execution, quality, and seek feedback!

– Coach Art Perry –

Rutgers, UConn, Delaware State, American, Maryland, Washington Wizards

Developing the Player Within

Skill development and player development does not simply refer to the ability to perform different moves with the ball. Neither does it refer only to the improvement we seek in field goal percentage and assist-to-turnover ratio. There are many mental skills to be developed on the court as well as character traits to develop for everywhere else. Sport and Performance Psychologist, Michael Gervais frequently reminds the audience of his Finding Mastery podcast:

"You can only train three things: Your body, your craft and your mind."

The drill portion of this journal is designed to help you train your craft – basketball skills. This is found in your practice plan for each day. The second portion of your daily routine will address training your mind—not only for performance on the court but also for performance in life. This part requires your response to thought-provoking questions after each training session. The third part, "Training your Body," will only be a small portion of this journal but will be extensively addressed in a future project related to strength and conditioning.

This chapter will breakdown the daily components of training your inner person. But first,

What Do You Want?

What is that thing that keeps you up at night, that thing you think about when you wake up in the morning? When something comes up in your schedule, you immediately think about how it will affect this thing. What is it? It is that place out there that you are running towards. And the closer you get, the more you want it. As one sociology teacher asked his class "What is that thing that you would never give up, even if I offered you ten million dollars today if you quit it and never did it again?" That thing. What is it?

There is a good chance, since you are reading this, that basketball is that thing for you. And if it isn't, it's pretty close. But here is the point: In the end, everyone gets what they want. Not immediately and not always easily, but eventually you will end up with what you want. Now obviously, there are limits to that statement. Just because you want to be president doesn't mean you will become president but it is very likely that you will end up in politics. And all along the course of your life, you will be making decisions and sacrifices to get what you want. You take political science courses, you volunteer during your free time, you pay attention to the debates and elections. Everything you do is a stepping stone on the way to your destination. Now the outcome, whether or not you become president or a senator or governor, it not something you can control. But what you can control are the decisions, the effort, the focus and sacrifices you make along the way. That is the training. And it is driven by what you want. Your purpose. Your passion.

So, the question you must ask yourself is this: "Do I want to be a great basketball player?" Someone else wanting it for you will not be enough. Do YOU want it? And if so, are you willing to lock in every day to make sure you are taking steps to reach your destination? What about days when you are tired or angry? What about when it is cold or raining? What about those days when things just go bad? Will you be locked-in on those days? How will you perform on those days?

My Story: Training the Player Within

As a basketball coach I spend most of my time coaching the mind of my players. I know that if our minds are not ready, we are not ready. And the best players always perform at their best when they are mentally locked in. Likewise, a mantra for the New Zealand All Black rugby team is "Keep a cool head"

"In any game played with the body, it is the head that counts most. Keep a cool head. Maintain clarity under pressure" - From James Kerr's book, Legacy

You can only keep a cool head when you are very clear about your purpose or goals.

As a team we discuss our team goals at the beginning of the year and constantly speak about them all season long. We ask ourselves if our effort and attitude is where it needs to be for us to accomplish our goals. We encourage one another to stay locked in, to stay the course and to press on. When things go bad, we say, "Play the next play." It is our reminder to not focus on the past which we can't control but to deal with the possession in front of us. We learn to deal with adversity by referring back to our foundational purpose or what the Navy Seals call their "Set Point" (Divine, 35-45).

In this journal I have broken your mental training into three parts: 1) purpose, 2) self-awareness, and 3) accountability. You will be required to speak to these things every day of your training. They are designed to keep you grounded. You must always know where you are, where you want to be and what you must do to get there.

Purpose - Stay Locked In

It is vital that you have purpose in life. What do you want to be? Or better yet, WHO do you want to be? Simon Sinek tells us that everything we do "starts with why." Why do you do what you do? It is important to keep your "why" in mind during your training. The "Locked In" portion of your journal is designed for you to think about why you are working so hard and what you are working toward becoming. Do not take this lightly. Examine your heart. Allow your desire and imagination to direct your steps. Be faithful with everything that has been given to you and maximize your potential. Stay focused and don't be moved away from your purpose.

Self-Awareness

You must know who you are. This world is full of people that don't know who they are and are just copying what others do. You don't have to be that way. Think often about who you are and who you want to become—then close the gap everyday. But in order to know how to bridge the gap, you must first know where you are in your development.

This will require SELF-evaluation—which is the best kind of evaluation. It will also require honesty and acceptance. You will have to look inward with an honest heart and evaluate who you are as a person and a player. Then you must accept that truth. This does not mean you have to stay that way; it only means that it is your starting point that day. Daily self-evaluation enables you to see how far you have grown and what you have to do next to reach your desired destination.

Accountability

In this section you will be asked to look at six areas of your life that are more about you as a person. But remember that who you are as a person will be revealed in competition sooner or later. Those six areas are: nutrition, sleep, character, responsibility, toughness, and attitude.

Nutrition. The further you progress as an athlete, the more important your nutrition will become. At the higher levels of competition, the difference between players is very small. Everything matters. If you have been eating unhealthy foods, you will grow sluggish in the final moments when you need your body the most. You wouldn't put bad fuel in a high performance sports car, so don't put bad food into your body.

Sleep. As an athlete you often push your body to it's limits. And your body will need time to recover and build muscle so it can adapt to the demands you are placing upon it. This happens when your body is at rest. Sleep will be vital to your overall health and performance. In this section you will be asked to constantly hold yourself accountable to getting a good amount of rest.

Character is often described as "who you are when no one is watching." In this section you will be challenged to "love your neighbor as you love yourself" and keep in mind that your family is your closest "neighbor." Your family and friends will make sacrifices to support you in your dream-chasing. It is right for you to show daily appreciation and to support them in their endeavors too.

Responsibility. Responsibility is made up of two words: response and ability. Wherever there is a need and you have the ability to respond to that need, you should. You may have chores, friends, family, pets, schoolwork, a job and other things that require your attention and effort. Be someone who is known for handling his or her business. Be someone that others can depend on.

Toughness. Let's be clear on this point: If you want to make it through this life successfully, you are going to have to be tough. You must be able to do what is required no matter how you feel about it. You must do your job every single time no matter what forces of opposition exist. Toughness requires resilience and focus.

Attitude. It is not just about getting the work done. It is also about the manner in which you do it. Do your work with joy. Go after your dreams with intensity and enthusiasm. Your attitude will be contagious to your teammates, good or bad. Learn to enjoy the work and embrace the challenge. Attitude has to do with your mindset during the performance. And your mindset is often reflected by your body language. Hanging your head or losing your cool reflects a defeated attitude, whereas a good attitude will almost always be optimistic. As legendary coach Pete Carroll says, "I just don't think something bad will happen. No matter how bad it gets, I just think: Okay, here we go, something good is about to happen." Guard your mind to only think the best things. Throw out defeated thoughts and replace them with thoughts of hope. Instead of thinking "we are going to lose this game" think "we are about to make a memorable comeback."

**Finally, brethren,
whatever things are true,
whatever things are noble,
whatever things are just,
whatever things are pure,
whatever things are lovely,
whatever things are of good report,
if there is any virtue and
if there is anything praiseworthy—
meditate on these things.**

Philippians 4:8

30 Days of Development

ach day will consist of a practice plan and a response page. You will complete the drills listed in the practice plan and follow that by reflecting on your work and performance.

The thirty days are broken up into three phases. Each phase will be progressively more demanding than the prior. You are expected to give a maximum effort in each drill and thoughtful answers in the responses. Remember this is for you. Own your development!

Sample Practice Plan

The practice plan is to be followed like a recipe, rather than treated like a menu. Follow the plan step by step and you WILL improve. Pick and choose only some of the drills and there is no guarantee. The practice plan is progressive and lays a foundation of fundamentals while also adding some room for challenge and creativity.

The practice plan starts with a thought for the day to get you in a frame of mind to work. You will then follow the plan from top to bottom. The drills are broken up into categories so you will know the focus and purpose of each drill. Some of the drills will have a score or time that should be recorded. In the back of the journal is a Record Book where you are to write down the first score you received in each drill or challenge as well as your personal best (you will be re-writing that one frequently).

Sample Response Page

The response page is to be completed after each workout. These are designed to keep you focused on your development as a player and person. Don't just fill them out to get the task done. Give deep thought to your responses and use all of the space.

Some of the sections will have multiple questions. These are to prime your thinking. You do not need to answer every single one. Let the questions marinate for a minute or two and then respond.

Other Suggestions

After you have completed the day's session, take a look at what is expected the next day. Some of the drills will absolutely require a rebounder/passer. If you know that you will not have anyone available, simply adjust the drill the best you can or substitute it for something comparable. The drills requiring another person will be labeled as such on the practice plan.

Look at the following Sample Pages to get a better feel for each day's practice.

Day Number

Every day you will find some "mind candy" here. This is in order to get your attention set on the task at hand and remind you why you have set out on this journey.

Practice Plan

You can plan on spending between 45-60 minutes each day working on your game. The practice will be broken down into key elements that you can work one individually. The allotted times are rough estimates of how many minutes each drill should take, based on my experience, to give you an idea of the length of each segment.

- ☐ <u>Vitamins</u>: (10min) These are the things that we will do everyday to warmup and get you competing and focused right away.
- ☐ <u>Defense</u>: (5min) Mindset, footwork and effort are key when training for defense. It is always good to hit this first.
- ☐ <u>Ball Handling</u>: (10min) The goal here is to get your hands ultra familiar with the ball. When the ball is in your hands you must be so comfortable and confident with it that when you are being trapped you will be able to calmly maneuver and pivot to find your place of attack.
- ☐ <u>Dribbling</u>: (10min) Drills using the bounce to get to your desired spots on the floor.
- ☐ <u>Finishing</u>: (10min) Utilizing various ways to score at the rim or in the paint.
- ☐ <u>Shooting</u>: (15min) Combination of spot shooting, shooting off the dribble, and shooting off the move.
- ☐ <u>Footwork</u>: (10min) Footwork is a subtle skill that is always SEEN in the best players but not always identified.

SAMPLE DAY

Locked In:

Here you will be prompted to think and write about what you want to accomplish and why you want to accomplish it.

____

____

____

Self Aware:

Here you will be prompted to identify your strengths, weaknesses, areas of improvement and interests.

____

____

____

Accountable:

Here you will check some boxes and evaluate yourself in the following areas. Did you handle your business?

- ☐ Nutrition
- ☐ Sleep
- ☐ Character
- ☐ Responsibility
- ☐ Toughness
- ☐ Attitude

GROWTH

FOR EVERY HILL I'VE HAD TO CLIMB
FOR EVERY STONE THAT BRUISED MY FEET
FOR ALL THE BLOOD AND SWEAT AND GRIME
MY HEART SINGS BUT A GRATEFUL SONG –
    THESE WERE THE THINGS THAT MADE ME STRONG

FOR ALL THE HEARTACHES AND THE TEARS
FOR ALL THE ANGUISH AND THE PAIN
FOR GLOOMY DAYS AND FRUITLESS YEARS
AND FOR THE HOPES THAT LIVED IN VAIN
I DO GIVE THANKS FOR NOW I KNOW –
    THESE WERE THE THINGS THAT HELPED ME GROW!

TIS NOT THE SOFTER THINGS IN LIFE
THAT STIMULATES MAN'S WILL TO STRIVE
BUT BLEAK ADVERSITY AND STRIFE
DO MOST TO KEEP MAN'S WILL ALIVE
O'ER ROSE STREWN PATHS THE WEAKLINGS CREEP –
    BUT BRAVE HEARTS DARE TO CLIMB THE STEEP.

– L. E. THAYER –

Phase One

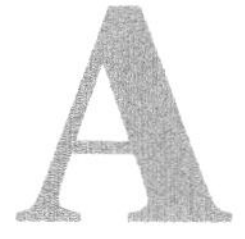A nd here we go! Nearly every drill will be new to you. That is to be understood. Do your very best. If it is your first time doing the drill, be sure to record your first attempt in the Record Book in the back. Aim for growth, not perfection.

Let me say congratulations on taking your first step toward growing as a basketball player. You obviously love the game and are committed to mastering your skills. Take a second to think of all the greats who have gone before you. Think of the sacrifices they made. Think of the paths they have carved out for you. Think of the innovative styles they have brought to this game. All of that takes curiosity, courage and grueling work. This practice floor is a court of honor that you are about to step on. Honor the game by giving your very best every day. You will find some of the same joy and satisfaction that those greats have found.

Day One

Often times the most difficult step is the first one. There is no momentum. There is hesitation. There is doubt. "Can I do it?" Today, throw all those doubts away like the impostors that they are. Today, you are starting something new. Bring it!

Practice Plan

<u>Vitamins</u>: (10min)

☐ Finger Taps, Ball Wraps, V-Dribbles

☐ Get 50   Total Misses: _____________

<u>Defense</u>: (5min)

☐ In and Out Shuffle

☐ Lane Shuttle   Time: _____________

<u>Dribble Attack</u>: (10min)

☐ Breakdown Drills

<u>Finishing</u>: (10min)

☐ Level One Finishes

<u>Shooting</u>: (20min)

☐ 1-Hand Form Shooting

☐ 2-Hand Form Shooting

☐ Midrange Challenge   Time: _____________

<u>Footwork</u>: (10min)

☐ Jab Series Breakdown

Free Throws in a Row   Total: _____________

Can't Miss Two (Midrange)   Total Makes : _____________

Locked In:

Write down what you want for yourself in terms of basketball. What do you want to be able to do? What team do you want to make? What player do you want to be like?

Self Aware:

What drills were the most challenging for you? Were you able to struggle through it? What can you improve on?

Accountable:

Did you handle your business today? Check the boxes of areas where you were able take a step forward in your development.

- ☐ Nutrition
- ☐ Sleep
- ☐ Character
- ☐ Responsibility
- ☐ Toughness
- ☐ Attitude

Day Two

Day one is under your belt. Now it's time to develop some momentum. Some of the drills will be repeats. See if you can improve on them from yesterday.

Practice Plan

<u>Vitamins</u>: (10min)

☐ Finger Taps, Ball Wraps, V-Dribbles

☐ Get 50   Total Misses: _______________

<u>Defense</u>: (5min)

☐ Lane Slides   Time: _______________

☐ Lane Shuttle   Time: _______________

<u>Dribble Attack</u>: (10min)

☐ Breakdown Drills

<u>Finishing</u>: (10min)

☐ Level One Finishes

<u>Shooting</u>: (15min)

☐ Arc Shooting

☐ Midrange Challenge   Time: _______________

<u>Footwork</u>: (10min)

☐ Jab Series Breakdown

☐ Make 3   Time: _______________

Free Throws in a Row   Total: _______________

Can't Miss Two (Midrange)   Total Makes: _______________

PHASE ONE

Locked In:

Name one player you would like to play like? What do you like about their game? What would you change or add? What do you know about their path to success?

____

____

____

Self Aware:

How did you do today? Did you feel more comfortable than yesterday?

____

____

____

Accountable:

Did you handle your business today? Check the boxes of areas where you were able take a step forward in your development.

☐ Nutrition   ☐ Responsibility

☐ Sleep   ☐ Toughness

☐ Character   ☐ Attitude

PHASE ONE

Day Three

Remember that basketball is a game. It is to be enjoyed. Work as hard as you can to improve but make sure you have fun doing it. Enjoy the process. Crave the results.

Practice Plan

<u>Vitamins</u>: (10min)

☐ Form Shooting

☐ Make 7   Distance: ___________

<u>Defense</u>: (10min)

☐ Full Court Zig-Zag

☐ Box Drill   Time: ___________

<u>Dribble Attack</u>: (10min)

☐ In the Trench

<u>Finishing</u>: (5min)

☐ Interior Finishes

<u>Shooting</u>: (10min)

☐ Midrange Challenge   Time: ___________

☐ Elevator Shooting   Time: ___________

<u>Footwork</u>: (10min)

☐ On the Move Series

Free Throws in a Row   Total: ___________

Can't Miss Two (Midrange)   Total Makes: ___________

Locked In:

Write down three goals. One for this week. One for this month. One for this year.

____

____

____

Self Aware:

On a scale of 1-10 rate yourself on how hard you worked today during your practice session. Try to give an explanation of your rating (either good or bad).

____

____

____

Accountable:

Rank these categories from 1-6. #1 is your strongest and #6 is your biggest area for improvement.

☐ Nutrition ☐ Responsibility

☐ Sleep ☐ Toughness

☐ Character ☐ Attitude

Day Four

Take care of your body. As an athlete, your body is vital to your success and accomplishing your goals. The phrase "no days off" means don't be a slacker but sometimes the day requires rest and recovery...don't be afraid to take a day off.

Practice Plan

<u>Vitamins</u>: (10min)

☐ Form Shooting

☐ Make 7 Range Finder   Distance: _____________

<u>Defense</u>: (5min)

☐ Line Drills

☐ Lane Slides   Time: _____________

<u>Dribble Attack</u>: (20min)

☐ Dribble Breakdown Series

☐ Blender Challenge

<u>Finishing</u>: (5min)

☐ Level One Finishing Series

<u>Shooting</u>: (10min)

☐ Sixes   Time: _____________

☐ Make 3   Time: _____________

<u>Footwork</u>: (10min)

☐ On the Move Series

Free Throws in a Row   Total: _____________

Can't Miss Two (Midrange)   Total Makes: _____________

Locked In:

If a college or NBA coach watched my training session today, they would be impressed by my...

____

____

____

Self Aware:

On a scale of 1-10 rate your love for the game of basketball. What do you love most?

____

____

____

Accountable:

Grade yourself. A, B, C, D, F. Are you on the honor roll of intangibles?

- ☐ Nutrition
- ☐ Sleep
- ☐ Character

- ☐ Responsibility
- ☐ Toughness
- ☐ Attitude

Day Five

Starting today, you will be adding "Movement Skills" to every workout. You will find that it will help you recover faster and reduce soreness in your muscles. Most players incorporate these into their pre-game, pre-practice routine.

Practice Plan

<u>Vitamins</u>: (10min)

☐ Movement Skills

☐ Make 7 Range Finder   Distance: _______________

<u>Defense</u>: (5min)

☐ Line Drills

☐ In & Out Shuffle

<u>Dribble Attack</u>: (20min)

☐ Dribble Breakdown Series

☐ Blender Challenge

<u>Finishing</u>: (10min)

☐ Interior Finishes

<u>Shooting</u>: (10min)

☐ Sixes   Time: _______________

☐ Make 3   Time: _______________

<u>Footwork</u>: (10min)

☐ On the Move Series

Free Throws in a Row   Total: _______________

Can't Miss Two (Midrange)   Total Makes: _______________

Locked In:

If a college or NBA coach watched my training session today, they would be would want me on their team because...

Self Aware:

Honestly, how do you measure up against other players your age? Name a player who is better than you and one player you could beat in one on one right now. (Invite them both to play!)

Accountable: Nutrition

What did you eat today that did NOT come out of a package?

Day Six

Great basketball players give 100% of their effort and attitude. They approach their work with courage, enthusiasm and passion. If that's who you want to be then BRING IT! Everyday!

Practice Plan

<u>Vitamins</u>: (10min)

☐ Movement Skills

☐ Get 50   Total Misses: ___________

<u>Defense</u>: (5min)

☐ In & Out Shuffle

☐ Box Drill   Time: ___________

<u>Dribble Attack</u>: (10min)

☐ V-Dribble Series

☐ 2-Ball Series

<u>Finishing</u>: (8min)

☐ Level One Finishing

<u>Shooting</u>: (12min)

☐ Arc Shooting

☐ Elevator   Time: ___________

☐ Make 3   Time: ___________

<u>Footwork</u>: (10min)

☐ Squaring Up Series

Free Throws in a Row   Total: ___________

Can't Miss Two (Midrange)   Total Makes: ___________

Locked In:

Think about where you are and where you want to end up. Label some mile-markers along the way. These are smaller goals along the way to your larger goal (your destination).

Where I am: ____

Mile Marker: ____

Mile Marker: ____

Destination: ____

Self Aware:

What have you improved on so far in your training? How can you tell?

____

____

____

Accountable: Nutrition

Check the boxes. What have you eaten today? A balanced diet is the goal. Limit the number of sweets and snacks.

☐ Fruits

☐ Vegetables

☐ Grains/Breads/Cereal

☐ Protein - meats, eggs

☐ Dairy - milk, cheese

☐ Sweets/Snacks

Day Seven

Give great attention to the details in life. Refuse to be sloppy about your work. Anything worth doing is worth doing well. Remember, everything matters...small things, big things, other things...they all add up.

Practice Plan

<u>Vitamins</u>: (10min)

☐ Movement Skills

☐ Make 7 Range Finder   Distance: _____________

<u>Defense</u>: (5min)

☐ Full Court Zig Zag

☐ Lane Shuttle   Time: _____________

<u>Dribble Attack</u>: (20min)

☐ Dribble Circles

☐ Dribble Breakdown Series

<u>Finishing</u>: (10min)

☐ Interior Finishes

☐ Level One Finishes

<u>Shooting</u>: (10min)

☐ Sixes   Time: _____________

<u>Footwork</u>: (10min)

☐ On the Move Series

Free Throws in a Row   Total: _____________

Can't Miss Two (Midrange)   Total Makes: _____________

Locked In:

What things are obstacles to you achieving your goals? List the things that you may need to "cut" from your life.

____

____

____

Self Aware:

It will be important in your life to precisely identify those things that you are good at. Write them down. Don't be shy.

____

____

____

Accountable: Nutrition

The rule, "eat for fuel, not taste" will help you choose foods. What did you eat today? Circle the best sources of fuel.

____

____

____

Day Eight

If first is available, why settle for second? If winning is an option, why not do just that? Prepare today for the victories you want to have in the future.

Practice Plan

<u>Vitamins</u>: (10min)

☐ Movement Skills

☐ Taps, Wraps, Form Shooting

<u>Defense</u>: (5min)

☐ Lane Slides   Time: _______________

☐ Lane Shuttle   Time: _______________

<u>Dribble Attack</u>: (20min)

☐ V-Dribble Series

☐ 2-Ball Series

☐ Dribble Circles

☐ Blender

<u>Finishing</u>: (6min)

☐ Level One Finishes

<u>Shooting</u>: (10min)

☐ Midrange Challenge   Time: _______________

<u>Footwork</u>: (10min)

☐ Steve Alford Challenge   Win/Loss: _______________

Free Throws in a Row   Total: _______________

Can't Miss Two (Midrange)   Total Makes: _______________

Locked In:

Write down your top three goals for next season.

Self Aware:

Think about your favorite/most effective offensive move. You must master it. Write down a few ways you can make this an "automatic" and "go-to" move.

Accountable: Nutrition

What are your favorite healthy foods? Remember these next time you go shopping. Make a list of fruits/veggies that you like. Remember them when you or a parent goes shopping.

Day Nine

There are 1,440 minutes in a day. If each of those minutes were a dollar that you get to keep if you use it wisely or lose if you waste it...how would you "spend" your day?

Practice Plan

<u>Vitamins</u>: (10min)
- ☐ Movement Skills
- ☐ Taps, Wraps, Form Shooting

<u>Defense</u>: (5min)
- ☐ Full Court Zig Zag
- ☐ Box Drill   Time: _______________

<u>Dribble Attack</u>: (20min)
- ☐ Dribble Circles
- ☐ 20/20/20   Time: _______________
- ☐ Breakdown Series

<u>Finishing</u>: (6min)
- ☐ Mount Zion   Total Points _______________

<u>Shooting</u>: (10min)
- ☐ Arc Shooting
- ☐ Elevator Shooting   Time: _______________
- ☐ Sixes   Time: _______________

<u>Footwork</u>: (10min)
- ☐ On the Move Series

Free Throws in a Row   Total: _______________
Can't Miss Two (Midrange)   Total Makes: _______________

Locked In:

What do you have to do this month to ensure you reach your goals next season?

____

____

____

Self Aware:

Spend some extra time studying someone who has mastered "your" move. Watch clips of them performing it. What can you adopt from them to improve your execution of it?

____

____

____

Accountable: Sleep

How many hours of sleep did you get last night? ____________.

Do you feel rested? __________.

Are you more of a night owl or early bird? ____________.

Day Ten

Focus on what you can control, not what you cannot control. You can't control the outcome of a game, season, or life...but you can control your preparation and work ethic.

Practice Plan

<u>Vitamins</u>: (10min)

☐ Movement Skills

☐ Get 50   Total Misses: ___________

<u>Defense</u>: (5min)

☐ In & Out Shuffle

☐ Lane Slides   Time: ___________

<u>Dribble Attack</u>: (20min)

☐ Dribble Circles

☐ 20/20/20   Time: ___________

☐ Breakdown Series

<u>Finishing</u>: (6min)

☐ Level One Finishes

<u>Shooting</u>: (10min)

☐ Arc Shooting

☐ Elevator Shooting   Time: ___________

☐ Midrange Challenge   Time: ___________

<u>Footwork</u>: (10min)

☐ Steve Alford Front Pivot   Win/Loss: ___________

Free Throws in a Row   Total: ___________

Can't Miss Two (Midrange)   Total Makes: ___________

Locked In:

What skills would have to refine or improve in order to play at the next level?

____

____

____

Self Aware:

What is the greatest achievement of your athletic life?

____

____

____

Accountable: Sleep

How many hours of sleep did you get last night? _______________ .
What do you think would be the impact of getting better rest each night?

____

____

____

Phase Two

You must develop at your own pace. Do not compare your development to others. Growing your skills is about mastering the fundamentals and then building upon them. The world's best players have masterful control of fundamental skills and as a result, are able to use them in multi-step combinations.

If you are struggling with any portion of Phase One, bring it with you. Add it as part of your warmup routine for Phase Two. Don't let pride get in the way of your development. Have enough self-awareness and humility to say, "I can't do this as well as I would like to. I'm going to stick with it until I am satisfied." Take control! Own your development! Focus on mastering each area of your game. Work on it until you've got it...then work on improving it some more.

ALWAYS A WAY

There is always a way to rise, my lad, always a way to advance, but the road that leads to Mount Success, does not pass by the way of chance; it goes through the stations of work and strive, through the valley of persevere; and the man that succeeds while others fail, must be willing to pay most dear. For there's always a way to fall, my lad, always a way to slide; and the men you find at the foot of the hill, all sought for an easy ride. And so on and up, though the road be rough, and the storms come thick and fast; there is room at the top for the fellow who tries, and victory comes at last.

– Councillor –

Day Eleven

Today is the start of phase two. This means we will be adding some new drills and progressing into some more difficult movements. Embrace the challenge. You will get the hang of it.

Practice Plan

<u>Vitamins</u>: (10min)

☐ Movement Skills

☐ Dribble Attack Breakdown Series

☐ Form Shooting

<u>Defense</u>: (5min)

☐ Line Drills

☐ Kentucky Stomps

<u>Dribble Attack</u>: (20min)

☐ Panther Series - 2s & 3s   Time: __________

☐ Panther Series - Ironman   Time: __________

<u>Finishing</u>: (6min)

☐ Level Two Finishes

<u>Shooting</u>: (10min)

☐ Make 3   Time: __________

☐ Sixes Off the Dribble   Time: __________

☐ Make 7 Range Finder   Distance: __________

<u>Footwork</u>: (10min)

☐ Post Move Series

☐ Free Throws in a Row   Total: __________

☐ Can't Miss Two (Midrange)   Total Makes: __________

PHASE TWO

Locked In:

Every time you join a new team or get a new coach the practices and drills will be different. How is your patience in learning new things?

Self Aware:

How did you do with the new drills? Anything new will be challenging until you become familiar with it. How is your mental approach to new things?

Accountable: Sleep

How many hours of sleep did you get last night? _____________ .
What routine can you develop for settling down at night?

Day Twelve

You must prepare for greatness. Prepare for the opportunity so that when it arises you are ready to perform. If you wait for the opportunity to arise, it will be too late. Do your work early!

Practice Plan

<u>Vitamins</u>: (10min)

☐ Movement Skills

☐ 20/20/20   Time: _____________

☐ 2-Ball Series

<u>Defense</u>: (5min)

☐ Kentucky Stomps

☐ Box Drill   Time: _____________

<u>Dribble Attack</u>: (20min)

☐ Dribble Circles

☐ Panther Series - 4x   Time: _____________

☐ Panther Series - Burnout   Reps: _____________

<u>Finishing</u>: (6min)

☐ Interior Finishes

☐ Level Two Finishes

<u>Shooting</u>: (10min)

☐ Sixes Off the Dribble   Time: _____________

☐ NBA Shooting (x3)   Scores: _____________

<u>Footwork</u>: (10min)

☐ Jab Series

Free Throws in a Row   Total: _____________

Can't Miss Two (Midrange)   Total Makes: _____________

Locked In:

Clearly state a basketball goal in one sentence. "I will..." Make sure it is specific, measurable and achievable.

Self Aware:

Do you fear failure? Try to define what that fear is? Not measuring up? Letting someone down? Being labeled? Now, how can you overcome that temptation? How can your mindset be changed?

Accountable: Sleep

How many hours of sleep did you get last night? _____________. What is your morning routine? What gets you up and gets you going?

Day Thirteen

When you want to stop, when you want to quit, when you want to lay down and say, "That's it!" remember that growth doesn't come at the end; it's what happens now, so let's go again!

Practice Plan

Vitamins: (10min)

- ☐ Movement Skills
- ☐ V-Dribble Series
- ☐ Blender

Defense: (6min)

- ☐ Lane Shuttle   Time: ___________
- ☐ Perimeter Closeout

Dribble Attack: (10min)

- ☐ In the Trench
- ☐ Jordan Attack - Doubles   Times: ___________
- ☐ Jordan Attack - Combos   Times: ___________

Finishing: (15min)

- ☐ Lillard Layups
- ☐ Level Two Finishes

Shooting: (10min)

- ☐ Holy Cross   Takes/Makes: ___________
- ☐ 50 in 3 (x2)   Makes: ___________

Footwork: (10min)

- ☐ Post Moves Series
- ☐ Offensive Rebounding Series

Free Throws in a Row   Total: ___________

Can't Miss Two (Midrange)   Total Makes: ___________

PHASE TWO

Locked In:

Clearly state an academic goal in one sentence. "I will…"

____

____

____

Self Aware:

How would others describe your playing style?

Coaches: ____________________________________

Teammates: ________________________________

Fans: ______________________________________

Accountable: Character

On a scale from 1-10 (10 being best) rate your performance the last 2 weeks:

Kindness: _______ *Patience:* _______

Compassion: _______ *Forgiveness:* _______

Honesty: _______ *Helpfulness:* _______

Encouragement: _______ *Comfort:* _______

Day Fourteen

In team sports differences are a source of strength. No team wants to have a bunch of clones. Be yourself. Work on your strengths. Accept your teammates and play to their strengths. The key is togetherness.

Practice Plan

<u>Vitamins</u>: (10min)

- ☐ Movement Skills
- ☐ Get 50   Total Misses: ___________
- ☐ Arc Shooting

<u>Defense</u>: (6min)

- ☐ Line Drills
- ☐ Perimeter Closeout

<u>Dribble Attack</u>: (10min)

- ☐ Panther Series - 2s & 3s   Time: ___________
- ☐ Panther Series - Ironman Time: ___________
- ☐ Panther Series - Taps   Time: ___________

<u>Finishing</u>: (10min)

- ☐ Lillard Layups
- ☐ Interior Finishes

<u>Shooting</u>: (10min)

- ☐ Make 7   Distance: ___________
- ☐ Elevator Shooting   Time: ___________
- ☐ NBA Shooting   Score: ___________

<u>Footwork</u>: (10min)

- ☐ Jab Series - 100 pt Challenge   Score: ___________

Free Throws in a Row   Total: ___________

Can't Miss Two (3 pt)   Total Makes: ___________

Locked In:

Some say that you are the average of the five people you spend the most time with. Who are your top five? Are they good for your development?

____

____

____

Self Aware:

Have you completed every task in the program so far? Have you done every part of the Movement Skills? Do you go max speed with the defensive assignments? Self-evaluate and reflect on how this will effect your progress as a player (either good or bad).

____

____

____

Accountable: Character

Check your top 3 areas for improvement:

Kindness: _________   Patience: _________

Compassion: _________   Forgiveness: _________

Honesty: _________   Helpfulness: _________

Encouragement: _________   Comfort: _________

PHASE TWO

Day Fifteen

Confidence is earned through putting in the work. Get as close as you can to the level of mastery of the skill and then...repetition, repetition, repetition. Earn the right to be confident!

Practice Plan

Vitamins: (20min)

- ☐ Movement Skills
- ☐ Dribble Circles
- ☐ Dribble Attack Breakdown Series

Defense: (6min)

- ☐ Kentucky Stomps
- ☐ Lane Shuttle   Time: ___________
- ☐ Box Drill   Time: ___________

Dribble Attack: (14min)

- ☐ Panther Series - 4x   Time: ___________
- ☐ Panther Series - Burnout   Reps: ___________
- ☐ Wing Attacks

Finishing: (10min)

- ☐ Interior Finishes

Shooting: (10min)

- ☐ 50 in 3   Makes: ___________

Footwork: (10min)

- ☐ Jab Series - 100pt Challenge   Score: ___________
- ☐ Steve Alford Challenge   Win/Loss: ___________
- ☐ Board Man Gets Paid   Score: ___________

Free Throws in a Row   Total: ___________

Can't Miss Two (3pt)   Total Makes: ___________

PHASE TWO

Locked In:

Your training sessions have been getting longer. How do you feel about this? The key is not the length of time but the level of focus and intensity. Are you able to keep your intensity up?

Self Aware:

What habits are starting to form in your training that you like? How will you plan to keep them going?

Accountable: Character

Write down one act of kindness that you will perform today for an adult (parent, grandparent, teacher etc.) Then...get to it.

Day Sixteen

The "Loaded Cannon" is named after one of my players who was determined to improve her shooting ability. One day after practice she asked if I would rebound for her. Without saying a word she went through a routine she had used for her own development and in the process created a new drill for her coach. That's taking ownership!

Practice Plan

<u>Vitamins</u>: (10min)

- ☐ Movement Skills
- ☐ 20/20/20
- ☐ 2-Ball Series

<u>Defense</u>: (6min)

- ☐ Line Drills
- ☐ Perimeter Closeout

<u>Dribble Attack</u>: (10min)

- ☐ Blender Challenge
- ☐ Wing Attacks

<u>Finishing</u>: (6min)

- ☐ Lillard Layups
- ☐ Interior Finishes

<u>Footwork</u>: (10min)

- ☐ Mount Zion

<u>Shooting</u>: (20min)

- ☐ Loaded Cannon

Free Throws in a Row

Can't Miss Two (3 pt)

Time: ___________

HELP WANTED

REBOUNDER FOR
"LOADED CANNON"

Score: ___________

Time: ___________

Total: ___________

Total Makes: ___________

Locked In:

Sports are fun, challenging, demanding and rewarding. What things can you learn from basketball that you can apply to the rest of your life?

Self Aware:

Write down how you generally deal with adversity. How do you handle losses? A bad test grade? Being insulted by a friend? Then, write down ways maintain your composure and be unconquerable!

Accountable: Character

Write down one act of kindness that you will perform for a peer (a sibling or friend or neighbor). Then...get to it

---

Day Seventeen

One of the marks of successful people is that they don't get too high in times of victory and they don't get too low in times of defeat. They stay the course and stick to the process. Celebrate the wins, learn from the losses and always "stay the course."

Practice Plan

Vitamins: (10min)

☐ Movement Skills

☐ In the Trench

☐ Form Shooting

Defense: (6min)

☐ Full Court Zig Zag

☐ Lane Slides   Time: ____________

Dribble Attack: (10min)

☐ V-Dribble Series

☐ Jordan Attack - Doubles   Times: ____________

☐ Jordan Attack - Combos   Times: ____________

Finishing: (10min)

☐ Level Two Finishing Series

Shooting: (20min)

☐ Arc Shooting

☐ Sixes Off The Dribble   Time: ____________

☐ Make 3   Time: ____________

☐ Holy Cross   Takes/Makes: ____________

Footwork: (10min)

☐ Pop-Curl-Fade   Score: ____________

Free Throws in a Row   Total: ____________

Can't Miss Two (3 pt)   Total Makes: ____________

> **"TOMORROW"**
>
> Remember this your lifetime through,
> Tomorrow there will be more to do.
> And failure waits for all who stay,
> With some success made yesterday.
> Tomorrow you must try once more
> And even harder than before.
>
> – John Wooden –

Locked In:

Greatness comes from doing the basic, foundational things better and more efficiently than everyone else. What are those basic things for you? What do you need to master?

Self Aware:

Write down how you generally deal with success. What do you do when you win? Ace a test? Achieve a goal? Now, in what ways can you both celebrate and stay the course?

Accountable: Responsibility

List your daily responsibilities. What is expected of you every day?

Day Eighteen

Before you learn how to win, you must learn how to lose. Losing has the potential to expose all of your weaknesses. If you are a player who makes excuses and blames others for a loss, you will never improve. Do not panic; do not despair. Simply observe, adjust and get to work.

Practice Plan

<u>Vitamins</u>: (10min)

☐ Movement Skills

☐ Dribble Breakdown Series

☐ Make 7   Distance: _____________

<u>Defense</u>: (6min)

☐ Lane Shuttle   Time: _____________

☐ Box Drill   Time: _____________

<u>Dribble Attack</u>: (20min)

☐ Panther Series - 2s & 3s   Time: _____________

☐ Panther Series - Ironman   Time: _____________

☐ Panther Series - 4x   Time: _____________

☐ Panther Series - Taps   Time: _____________

☐ Panther Series - Burnout   Reps: _____________

<u>Finishing</u>: (6min)

☐ Lillard Layups

<u>Footwork</u>: (10min)

☐ Board Man Gets Paid   Score: _____________

☐ Jab Series

<u>Shooting</u>: (20min)

☐ NBA Shooting   Score: _____________

Free Throws in a Row   Total: _____________

Can't Miss Two (3pt)   Total Makes: _____________

Locked In:

What is one thing you can do today that will make an immediate impact on your development?

Self Aware:

Do you love to win or hate to lose? Explain.

Accountable: Responsibility

Responsibility can be broken down into two words: Response + Ability. List things that you are NOT expected to do but you have the "ability" to do in order to "respond" to a need. Where can you help out more?

Day Nineteen

Be a curious person. Do whatever it takes to put yourself in a situation where you can see how good you are. Don't be afraid to test your limits, comforts and work capacity. Push yourself. Be curious about your potential.

Practice Plan

Vitamins: (10min)
- ☐ Movement Skills
- ☐ Dribble Circles
- ☐ Form Shooting

Defense: (6min)
- ☐ Line Drills
- ☐ Perimeter Closeout

Dribble Attack: (12min)
- ☐ Blender Challenge
- ☐ Wing Attacks

Finishing: (6min)
- ☐ Interior Finishes

Shooting: (20min)
- ☐ Arc Shooting
- ☐ Elevator Shooting   Time: __________
- ☐ Holy Cross   Takes/Makes: __________
- ☐ Sixes Off The Dribble   Time: __________

Footwork: (10min)
- ☐ Pop-Curl-Fade Challenge   Score: __________
- ☐ Steve Alford (Reverse Pivot)   Win/Loss: __________

Free Throws in a Row   Total: __________

Can't Miss Two (3 pt)   Total Makes: __________

Locked In:

What characteristics do you display in your training (while no one is watching) that you hope will be respected and imitated by your teammates when they see how you work?

Self Aware:

Think about when you are at your best on the court. What are the conditions? How was sleep? Meals? Attitude? What time of day? Etc.

Accountable: Responsibility

Responsible people are dependable people. What can you do to improve your dependability? (Example: I can tell my parents when I will be home)

Day Twenty

PHASE TWO

Colossians 3:23 says "And whatever you do, do it heartily, as unto the Lord and not unto men." WHATEVER you do, do it with all your heart. When you put forth that kind of effort you will be rewarded by the work itself; and you may even find the results you are looking for.

Practice Plan

<u>Vitamins</u>: (10min)

- ☐ Movement Skills
- ☐ 20/20/20   Time: __________
- ☐ Wrap Around Challenge   Reps: __________
- ☐ Make 7   Distance: __________

<u>Defense</u>: (5min)

- ☐ Full Court Zig Zag

<u>Dribble Attack</u>: (20min)

- ☐ V-Dribble Series
- ☐ Dribble Breakdown Series
- ☐ In the Trench

<u>Finishing</u>: (15min)

- ☐ Lillard Layups
- ☐ Level 1 Finishing Series
- ☐ Level 2 Finishing Series

<u>Footwork</u>: (10min)

- ☐ Mount Zion Challenge   Score: __________

<u>Shooting</u>: (min)

- ☐ Midrange Challenge   Time: __________
- ☐ 50 in 3   Score: __________
- ☐ Free Throws in a Row   Total: __________
- ☐ Can't Miss Two (3 pt)   Total Makes: __________

Locked In:

If you got called for to play in a tournament this weekend, would you be ready? What would you do differently how you've been training the past 19 days?

Self Aware:

Who is your biggest opponent? You or someone else? Why?

Accountable: Responsibility

"Handle your business" is a core component of responsibility. The next level is to help others handle their business. How can you do this today?

Phase Three

Y ou have come to the last phase of the program. These last ten days will have more drills per day but shouldn't take you much more time each day. Now that you have a good idea of what is involved, you should be able to get right to work.

Fight any urge to coast. When you see the finish line, speed up and sprint through it. Finish strong!

You will see a few new drills but not many. Don't forget to enter your first attempt in the record book in the back. Continue to update your personal bests as well. You should be seeing some growth and more confidence in your skills now. Keep it going.

If you have opportunities, use your newly acquired or refined skills in competition. One-on-one is best to work on personal skills but two-on-two, three-on-three, four-on-four and five-on-five games will also help you learn when it is appropriate to use them. You must improve your basketball IQ and team concepts through competition. Have fun and work hard! Don't hesitate. Don't doubt.

Let it fly!

THINKING

"As he thinks in his heart; so he is." (Proverbs 23:7)

If you think you are beaten, you are
    If you think you dare not, you don't
    If you like to win but think you can't
    It's almost a cinch you won't.

If you think you'll lose, you're lost
    For out in the world we find
    Success begins with a fellow's will
    It's all in the state of mind.

If you think you are out-classed, you are
    You've got to think high to rise
    You've got to be sure of yourself before
    You can ever win a prize.

Life's battles don't always go
    To the stronger or the faster man
    But sooner or later the man who wins
    Is the man who thinks he can.

– Walter D. Wintle –

Day Twenty-One

Today starts phase three. If you are sticking to the plan and giving maximum effort then you are getting better. That is the recipe. No secret drills necessary. Work hard at challenging drills that develop skills needed to compete–over and over and over!

Practice Plan

<u>Vitamins</u>: (10min)

☐ Movement Skills

☐ Get 50

☐ Form Shooting

<u>Defense</u>: (5min)

☐ Line Drills

<u>Dribble Attack</u>: (20min)

☐ Dribble Circles

☐ 2-Ball Series

☐ Blender Challenge

<u>Finishing</u>: (10min)

☐ Level 3 Finishing Series

☐ Board Man Gets Paid

<u>Footwork</u>: (10min)

☐ Post Move Series

<u>Shooting</u>: (20min)

☐ Loaded Cannon

☐ Free Throws in a Row

☐ Can't Miss Two (3 pt)

Total Misses: ___________

Score: ___________

Time: ___________

Total: ___________

Total Makes: ___________

PHASE THREE

Locked In:

You should be getting stronger and in better condition as a result of your training. If you can increase your strength and speed along with your skills you will become a better player. What do you do to train your body?

Self Aware:

Do you find yourself enjoying the work? Why or why not?

Accountable: Toughness

Toughness is the ability to do the next right thing no matter what. What prevents you from doing the next right thing? What things make you quit? Physical? Mental?

Day Twenty-Two

"Be comfortable being uncomfortable" (Tim Grover). When things get tough or frustrating or painful - most people quit. You must get to a place where you are comfortable being uncomfortable; where the things that make others quit, is familiar to you.

Practice Plan

<u>Vitamins</u>: (15min)

- ☐ Movement Skills
- ☐ V-Dribble Series
- ☐ Arc Shooting
- ☐ Make 7 Range Finder   Distance: ___________

<u>Defense</u>: (5min)

- ☐ Clockwork
- ☐ Box Drill   Time: ___________

<u>Dribble Attack</u>: (10min)

- ☐ Panther Series - 2s and 3s   Time: ___________
- ☐ Panther Series - Burnout   Reps: ___________
- ☐ Jordan Attack - Combos   Times: ___________

<u>Finishing</u>: (15min)

- ☐ Lillard Layups
- ☐ Level Three Finishing Series

<u>Footwork</u>: (10min)

- ☐ Jab Series - 100 pt Challenge   Score: ___________

<u>Shooting</u>: (10min)

- ☐ NBA Shooting   Score: ___________
- ☐ Holy Cross (2x)   Takes/Makes: ___________

Free Throws in a Row   Total: ___________

Can't Miss Two (3 pt)   Total Makes: ___________

Locked In:

The further you go in basketball, in school, in your career, the hard the work will become. The challenges will increase and those who can adapt and adjust while maintaining composure will succeed. What words will you tell yourself when those times come?

Self Aware:

What things on the basketball court make you uncomfortable? Certain defenses? Crowds? Important game?

Accountable: Toughness

List three ways that you can help your teammates develop toughness.

PHASE THREE

Day Twenty-Three

On of my assistant coaches always reminds me that pressure is a privilege. The fact that you feel the pressure means you are in a position to do something great. Learn to embrace and excel when the pressure is on. You are training for those moments.

Practice Plan

<u>Vitamins</u>: (10min)

- ☐ Movement Skills
- ☐ Dribble Breakdown Series
- ☐ Sixes (not for time)

<u>Defense</u>: (5min)

- ☐ Line Drills
- ☐ Clockwork

<u>Dribble Attack</u>: (15min)

- ☐ Panther Series - 4x   Time: ___________
- ☐ Panther Series - Ironman   Time: ___________
- ☐ Wing Attacks

<u>Finishing</u>: (15min)

- ☐ Level 1 Finishing Series
- ☐ Level 2 Finishing Series
- ☐ Level 3 Finishing Series

<u>Footwork</u>: (10min)

- ☐ On the Move Series

<u>Shooting</u>: (10min)

- ☐ Steve Alford (Reverse Pivot)   Win/Loss: ___________
- ☐ 50 in 3   Score: ___________
- Free Throws in a Row   Total: ___________
- Can't Miss Two (3 pt)   Total Makes: ___________

Locked In:

The most difficult time to quit is the first time. What does that mean to you? What happens the second time you want to quit?

Self Aware:

Michael Gervais always asks the question "Where does pressure come from?" Is it from you? Others? Expectations?

Accountable: Toughness

Rank your level of toughness today 1-10 (10 being the toughest) and explain why.

PHASE THREE

Day Twenty-Four

"True success is attained only through the satisfaction of knowing you did everything within the limits of your ability to become the very best that you are capable of being" (John Wooden).

Practice Plan

<u>Vitamins</u>: (10min)

☐ Movement Skills

☐ 20/20/20   Time: ___________

☐ Make 7 Range Finder   Distance: ___________

<u>Defense</u>: (5min)

☐ Perimeter Closeout

☐ Box Drill   Time: ___________

☐ Lane Shuttle   Time: ___________

<u>Dribble Attack</u>: (20min)

☐ Panther Series - Taps   Time: ___________

☐ Jordan Attack - Doubles   Times: ___________

☐ Jordan Attack - Combos   Times: ___________

<u>Finishing</u>: (15min)

☐ Interior Finishes

☐ Lillard Layups

<u>Footwork</u>: (10min)

☐ Post Move Series

☐ Mount Zion Challenge   Time: ___________

<u>Shooting</u>: (5min)

☐ Holy Cross   Takes/Makes: ___________

☐ 50 in 3   Total: ___________

Free Throws in a Row   Total: ___________

Can't Miss Two (3 pt)   Total Makes: ___________

Locked In:

Make a list of three people that you need to invite to play one-on-one—players that will challenge you, beat you. Fine tune your skills while playing in competitive one-on-one games. It will work wonders for your development.

Self Aware:

Development check-in: In what ways have you gotten better? What areas do you need to put more focus on?

Accountable: Attitude

There are two things you can always control: your effort and your attitude. Describe how your attitude has been during this program.

Day Twenty-Five

"Make each day your masterpiece" (John Wooden). You must treat each day as it might be your last. Then get to work at making it a day that you can look back on a say, "I was at my best today."

***Alert: A lot of shooting today. You will need a rebounder.

Practice Plan

<u>Vitamins</u>: (15min)

- ☐ Movement Skills
- ☐ Get 50
- ☐ Form Shooting

<u>Defense</u>: (5min)

- ☐ Line Drills
- ☐ Perimeter Closeout

<u>Dribble Attack</u>: (10min)

- ☐ Dribble Circles
- ☐ In the Trench

<u>Finishing</u>: (5min)

- ☐ Level 3 Finishing Series

<u>Footwork</u>: (10min)

- ☐ Next Level Jab Series

<u>Shooting</u>: (30min)

- ☐ Weber State License to Shoot
- ☐ Loaded Cannon

Total Misses: ___________

Total: ___________

Time: ___________

Free Throws in a Row   Total: ___________

Can't Miss Two (3 pt)   Total Makes: ___________

PHASE THREE

Locked In:

Chris Paul said that Russell Westbrook was one of the hardest guys to guard, not because of his athleticism but because "He would miss 8 straight shots and come down and shoot the 9th like he just made eight in a row." How well do you bounce back from "misses" in life?

Self Aware:

What kind of self talk do you use when shooting? Do you sigh and mope or do you say "C'mon, I got the next one"?

Accountable: Attitude

How do your teammates' attitudes during practice or a game affect you?

PHASE THREE

Day Twenty-Six

"You don't need to love the process, you just need to crave the results" (Tim Grover). Players who desperately want to improve, usually do.

Practice Plan

<u>Vitamins</u>: (10min)

☐ Movement Skills

☐ V-Dribble Series

☐ Arc Shooting

<u>Defense</u>: (10min)

☐ Clockwork

☐ Kentucky Stomps

☐ Box Drill   Time: ___________

<u>Dribble Attack</u>: (5min)

☐ Panther Series - 2s & 3s   Time: ___________

☐ Panther Series - 4x   Time: ___________

☐ Panther Series - Taps   Time: ___________

<u>Finishing</u>: (10min)

☐ Level 1 Finishing Series

☐ Level 2 Finishing Series

<u>Footwork</u>: (10min)

☐ Jab Series

☐ Next Level Jab Series

<u>Shooting</u>: (20min)

☐ NBA Shooting (2x)   Score: ___________

☐ Weber State License to Shoot Total: ___________

Free Throws in a Row   Total: ___________

Can't Miss Two (3 pt)   Total Makes: ___________

Locked In:

To "crave the results" you must have a clear idea of what those results are. Clearly state want you are striving to become.

____

____

____

Self Aware:

Grade yourself on your training so far. How was your attendance? Effort? Enthusiasm? Improvement?

____

____

____

Accountable: Attitude

What would it look like to have a good attitude on a basketball team? What things would a person with a good attitude do?

____

____

____

Day Twenty-Seven

Never allow your body to outgrow your spirit. As much as you are training your body and skill and mind, make sure you are filling your heart with good things. – It is most important.

Practice Plan

<u>Vitamins</u>: (10min)

- ☐ Movement Skills
- ☐ Arc Shooting

<u>Defense</u>: (10min)

- ☐ Line Drills
- ☐ Lane Shuttle (x2)   Best Time: ____________
- ☐ Perimeter Closeout

<u>Dribble Attack</u>: (10min)

- ☐ Panther Series - Ironman   Time: ____________
- ☐ Panther Series - 4x   Time: ____________
- ☐ Panther Series - Burnout   Time: ____________

<u>Finishing</u>: (10min)

- ☐ Interior Finishes
- ☐ Level 3 Finishing Series

<u>Footwork</u>: (15min)

- ☐ Board Man Gets Paid   Score: ____________
- ☐ Mount Zion Challenge   Score: ____________

<u>Shooting</u>: (20min)

- ☐ Sixes off the Dribble (no score)
- ☐ Make 3   Score: ____________
- ☐ 50 in 3   Score: ____________

Free Throws in a Row   Total: ____________

Can't Miss Two (3 pt)   Total Makes: ____________

Locked In:

To "crave the results" you must have a clear idea of what those results are. Clearly state want you are striving to become.

Self Aware:

The most successful people are those who master the ability to recover from failure. How well do you do this?

Accountable: Attitude

What would it look like to have a a good attitude on a basketball team? What things would a person do?

Day Twenty-Eight

Remember the work. Get a little bit better each day, each drill, each rep. Strive to constantly improve even if the improvement is in small amounts...they add up.

Practice Plan

<u>Vitamins</u>: (10min)

- ☐ Movement Skills
- ☐ Wrap Around Challenge   Reps: ___________
- ☐ 20/20/20   Time: ___________

<u>Defense</u>: (10min)

- ☐ Full Court Zig Zag
- ☐ Clock Work

<u>Dribble Attack</u>: (10min)

- ☐ Dribble Circles
- ☐ V-Dribble Series
- ☐ Jordan Attack - Combos   Time: ___________

<u>Finishing</u>: (10min)

- ☐ Interior Finishes
- ☐ Lillard Layups

<u>Footwork</u>: (15min)

- ☐ Squaring Up Series
- ☐ Steve Alford (Front Pivot)   Score: ___________

<u>Shooting</u>: (15min)

- ☐ Elevator   Time: ___________
- ☐ NBA Shooting   Score: ___________
- ☐ 50 in 3   Score: ___________

Free Throws in a Row   Total: ___________

Can't Miss Two (3 pt)   Total Makes: ___________

Locked In:

In a very real sense you cannot worry about tomorrow and you cannot worry about yesterday. You have to live today, today. What will you do today that will make a difference in someone else's life?

Self Aware:

Consider this past year. What was 1) the highlight, 2) the lowlight, and 3) the biggest surprise of your year?

Accountable:

Now that we have spent some time on each of the following specifically, check the boxes of the areas where you have improved as a person.

☐ Nutrition   ☐ Responsibility
☐ Sleep   ☐ Toughness
☐ Character   ☐ Attitude

Day Twenty-Nine

"The challenge is to always get improve, to always get better, even when you best. Especially when you are the best" (New Zealand All-Blacks Rugby Team). The greatest never stop improving.

Practice Plan

<u>Vitamins</u>: (10min)

☐ Make 7 Range Finder   Distance: _________

☐ 20/20/20   Time: _________

<u>Defense</u>: (10min)

☐ Box Drill   Time: _________

☐ Lane Shuttle   Time: _________

☐ Lane Slides   Time: _________

<u>Dribble Attack</u>: (10min)

☐ Panther Series - 2s & 3s   Time: _________

☐ Panther Series - 4x   Time: _________

☐ Jordan Attack - Combos   Time: _________

<u>Finishing</u>: (10min)

☐ Get 50   Total Misses: _________

<u>Footwork</u>: (15min)

☐ Jab Series - 100 pt Challenge   Score: _________

☐ Mount Zion Challenge   Score: _________

☐ Pop-Curl-Fade   Score: _________

☐ Steve Alford (Reverse Pivot)   Win/Loss: _________

<u>Shooting</u>: (20min)

☐ Make 3   Time: _________

☐ Midrange Challenge   Time: _________

Free Throws in a Row   Total: _________

Can't Miss Two (3 pt)   Total Makes: _________

Locked In:

Today and tomorrow are challenge days. Time to perform. Do the best you can. Write down the drills you want to win tomorrow.

____

____

____

Self Aware:

List your biggest 3 weaknesses and 1 way to improve them.

____

____

____

Accountable:

Grade yourself on these intangibles

☐ Nutrition   ☐ Responsibility
☐ Sleep   ☐ Toughness
☐ Character   ☐ Attitude

Day Thirty

Last Day - Best Day. In most situations only one team gets to finish the season with a win. Collect as many wins today as possible. Perform.

Practice Plan

<u>Vitamins</u>: (5min)

- ☐ Panther Series - Ironman   Time: __________
- ☐ Wrap Around Challenge   Time: __________

<u>Defense</u>: (5min)

- ☐ Box Drill   Time: __________
- ☐ Lane Shuttle   Time: __________

<u>Dribble Attack</u>: (5min)

- ☐ Panther Series - Taps   Time: __________
- ☐ Panther Series - Burnout   Time: __________
- ☐ Jordan Attack - Doubles   Time: __________

<u>Footwork</u>: (10min)

- ☐ Board Man Gets Paid   Score: __________

<u>Shooting</u>: (40min)

- ☐ Holy Cross   Takes/Makes: __________
- ☐ Elevator   Time: __________
- ☐ NBA Shooting   Score: __________
- ☐ 50 in 3   Score: __________
- ☐ Weber State License to Shoot   Score: __________
- ☐ Loaded Cannon

Free Throws in a Row   Total: __________

Can't Miss Two (3 pt)   Total Makes: __________

HELP WANTED

REBOUNDER

PHASE THREE

Locked In:

You have goals and you have dreams. A dream without the preparation and work ethic only becomes a nightmare. How will you ensure that you will continue to chase your dreams from here on?

Self Aware:

List your biggest three strengths and one way to master each of them.

Accountable:

Always hold yourself accountable to a high standard. Be a person that makes other better for having known you. Now, pick the top areas that need improvement and get to work.

☐ Nutrition   ☐ Responsibility
☐ Sleep   ☐ Toughness
☐ Character   ☐ Attitude

RECORD BOOK

It is important that you write down what you have accomplished. This is an objective way to determine if you have improved as a player. You will find that it will encourage you and build your confidence. Training isn't rocket science or some magical formula to improve as a person or player. If you simply identify the things you want to improve and form a strategy or program that will help you...you will get better. Here is your measuring tool. Did you get better?

DRILL	FIRST ATTEMPT	PERSONAL BEST
20/20/20		
50 in 3		
Board Man Gets Paid		
Box Drill		
Can't Miss Two Midrange		
Can't Miss Two 3 pt		
Elevator		
Free Throws in a Row		
Get 50		
Holy Cross		
Jab Series - 100 pt Challenge		
Jordan Attack - Combos		

Jordan Attack - Doubles		
Lane Shuttle		
Lane Slides		
Loaded Cannon		
Make 3		
Make 7 Range Finder (distance)		
Midrange Challenge		
Mount Zion Challenge		
NBA Shooting		
Panther Series - 2s & 3s		
Panther Series - 4x		
Panther Series - Burnout		
Panther Series - Ironman		
Panther Series - Taps		
Pop-Curl-Fade Challenge		
Sixes		
Sixes off the Dribble		
Steve Alford Front Pivot		
Steve Alford Reverse Pivot		
Weber State License to Shoot		
Wrap Around Challenge		

Final Words

It is not easy to train on your own. It takes a burning desire from WITHIN...within YOU. If you have completed this book and fulfilled the tasks contained in it, you have shown great determination. That sort of effort gets rewarded sooner or later. Sometimes this requires patience. Sometimes it requires the right circumstance. Nevertheless, you must stay resolved, focused and prepared to perform when the opportunity presents itself.

Aside from your personal skill development and training, there are some other things you can do to improve. First, you must challenge yourself and test your development against others—compete, as soon and as often as possible! Second, as an athlete you must train your body for competition with strength and conditioning work. So let's take a quick look at those two things.

Competition

There have always been players who could master drills and win skill challenges better than anyone but could not get those skills to translate to in-game competition. This is the primary work of coaches. They stay up at night thinking about creating drills to help their players develop the skills necessary in competition. Then they spend even more time trying to figure out how those skills will transfer into actual game play. This happens through focusing on using those skills in competition.

A basketball game is a performance.

Players must practice their performance. The best way to do this is by playing in focused, purposeful competitions. In the coaching world we call these "small-sided games." For example, after you have worked diligently on your Dribble Attack moves, call a friend over to play one on one and specifically work on the new moves you've added to your game. Or, after you have practiced "On the Move Shooting," call up more friends and play two on two or three on three. Practice coming off of screens for jumpers. Practice catching at the elbow and utilizing the Reverse Pivot Series. Practice your on-the-ball defense, then help in the gaps and drop to the help side. Practice performing these skills in live competition. Don't just resort to those same moves you've been doing for years. Try out some new things. Competition will quickly show you where you need to work.

Strength and Conditioning

Weight Room Myths	Weight Room Truths
- Messes up your shot	- Makes you stronger
- Makes you feel big/bulky	- Decreases chance of injury
- Makes you slow	- Makes you more confident
- Makes you less flexible	- Increases mental toughness

Jon Beck, Skills Coach

Do not be afraid to lift weights! Just make sure you are doing the right exercises and maintaining proper form. If possible, I recommend lifting all year long. I would certainly ease up a bit in-season but continue to strength train. Seek guidance from a certified functional strength coach prior to selecting a program.

Here are a few basic principles for strength and conditioning:
- Focus on movements, not muscles.
- If you lose perfect form, the set is done.
- You are training for performance on the court, not in the weight room.
- Force yourself to stay away from machines whenever possible. – Machines provide stability for you, do exercises where YOU are required to provide the stability.

Here are a few movements you should include:

MOVEMENT	OPTIONS	REASON	AVOID
Squat	Goblet (2 legs) Split (1 leg dom.)	Power, Sprinting	Heavy weight on back
Deadlift	Trap Bar Single Leg	Deceleration, Jumping Motion	Hunching over
Push	Push-ups Bench Press Overhead Press	Shoulder and chest strength	Heavy weight
Pull	Row Pull-up	Shoulder and core stability	Swinging arms and weak core
Core Stability	Side and Front Planks	Stability, body control	letting hips dip

You should also try to include plyometrics, which are explosive movements such as box jumps, tuck jumps, broad jumps or single leg jumps. For upper body this can include medicine ball throws.

Lastly, conditioning! Try to avoid long distance running. It doesn't allow full hip range of motion and often causes soreness from a lot of pounding for your feet and knees. Sprint! Try to sprint at top speed at least twice per week.

Any strength and conditioning work should be preceded by the "movement skills" warmup that you have done for your practices. For more information on strength and conditioning for basketball players go to www.FactorySportsDE.com.

Be Smart

You must think about how you will spend your time. Time is the greatest commodity. You cannot add an hour to your life and once an hour is up it is gone for ever. It is important that you don't waste your time when practicing. Make sure you are working on things that will translate into game performance. Do the move correctly and then do it over and over and over.

Remember: "Don't get bored with getting better."

When you play pick-up games think about what you need to improve– especially if it is a non-competitive game. Do you need to get in shape? Make sure you touch each baseline every possession. Do you need to work on attacking? Don't take any jump shots–only layups. Can you improve your rebounding? Try to grab every_single_board! Be smart and make those games work for you.

Lastly, make sure you sift through online videos and drills. As you have learned, you don't need a lot of extra gadgets or eight-part moves. Think about what actually works in games (particularly, what works for YOU) and practice those.

My Story

My basketball notebook and desire to improve took me to a good high school and college career. I think I maxed out my potential as a basketball player. I enjoyed the practice, the training, the work it took to compete at a high level. I am satisfied with the results.

Now I continue to share what I have learned and continue to learn about the game and about player development. I have been fortunate enough to train and coach several college basketball players. And yet, at our gym Factory Sports, we start with players full of promise at the ripe old age of five or so. We teach them right from the start to work hard and have fun.

...but it's not about me!

Time to Write Your Story

I took my notebook, developed as a player, wrote my story as a player and am still writing it as a coach. How will your story go? What experiences will you have while handling this leather ball? What stories will you tell when you are an adult teaching young people the lessons you learned? Whatever that story may be, I wish you well. Have no regrets. Own your development. And let it fly!

Sincerely yours,

Coach Woods

> **Visit**
>
> **www.FactorySportsDE.com**
>
> **to access the video library demonstrating the drills.**

The Drills Index

If you have any questions about these drills contact Coach Woods at www.FactorySportsDE.com

Take Your Vitamins

<u>Form Shooting</u> - with the ball in the middle of your hand as though you were carrying a tray of pizza, squat down and sit on an imaginary chair. Fully extended and reach as high as possible finishing on your toes with a strong follow through at the wrist. You should feel the ball touch your index and middle finger last. Feel free to include a small jump as you move away from the basket.

- 1-Hand - 10x at 5ft, 10ft, 15ft (free throw line), 20ft (3 pt)
- 2-Hand - same as above
- Make 7 Range Finder - 2-hand form shooting but you cannot move back unless you make 7/10. Where you leave off is your "range."

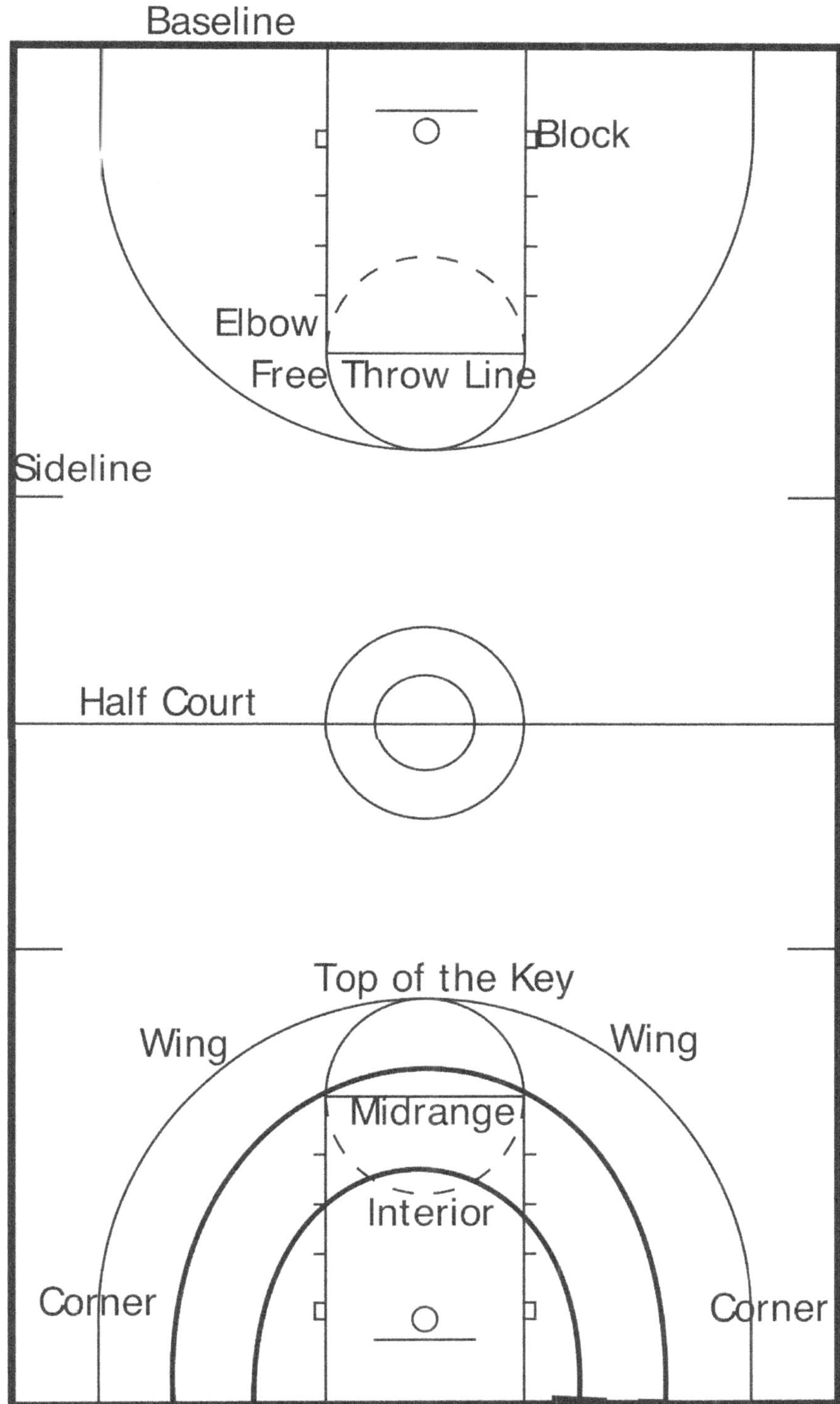

Baseline
Block
Elbow
Free Throw Line
Sideline
Half Court
Top of the Key
Wing
Wing
Midrange
Interior
Corner
Corner

<u>Get 50</u> - continuous shots alternating sides of the court. Make a total of 50 shots with as few misses as possible. Goals: MS = 20 misses, HS = 15 misses, College = 10 misses
- Make 10 "Mikans" - continuous layups under the rim jumping off inside foot and extending with outside arm
- Make 10 "Reverse Mikans" - same as above but with your back facing the baseline
- Make 10 "Drop Steps" - jumping off of two feet
- Make 10 "Bank Shots" - from about 8ft from the basket using the backboard
- Make 10 "Elbow Jumpers" - jump shots from the corners of the free throw line.

<u>Movement Skills</u> - with a tight core perform these drills designed to open up your joints for optimal movement and muscle activation. Designed for going to half court and back.
- Skips - forward then backward. Knee drive.
- High Knees - don't lean back. Drive knees waist high.
- Butt Kicks - bring heels to butt as you jog.
- Step and Slide - get low and wide in defensive stance, make stance wider (step) then slide trail foot to original stance. Move left 10x then right 10x.
- Shuffle - quicker version of step and slide. Defensive shuffle to the right then to the left.
- Back pedal - weight forward but moving backward (stay balanced so you don't fall backward).
- Backward run - same as above but standing taller and reaching back and grabbing the ground with your feet.
- Tuck Jumps - with no steps, swing your arms back as you squat then jump as high as possible bringing your knees to your chest in mid air. 10x

- Broad Jumps - with no steps, swing your arms back as you squat then jump as far as possible bringing feet forward for a balanced landing. 10x
- Lunge Matrix - start in a defensive stance and imagine you are standing on a clock. Lunge to one o'clock, three o'clock, five o'clock with right leg (3x each). Each time coming back to defensive stance. Hips down. With left leg lunge to eleven o'clock, nine o'clock, seven o'clock (3x each).
- Shoulder Taps - from pushup position maintaining a rigid core alternate tapping your left shoulder with your right hand and right shoulder with your left hand. 20 total taps.

<u>Taps</u> - with ball on fingertips rapidly tap it back and forth.
- 20x in front of your chest.
- 20x by your waist.
- 20x by your feet.
- 20x above your head.
- 20x rotating it one direction and 20x the other.

<u>Wrap Around Series</u> - with the ball in hand you will wrap the ball around your body as quickly as possible.
- 10x around your waist, switch directions, 10 more.
- 10x around your feet, switch directions, 10 more.
- 10x around your head, switch directions, 10 more.
- Tornado - around head, waist, feet, waist = 1. Do 10x and switch directions.
- Challenge - Wrap around your waist as many times as possible in 1 minute. Switch directions every 20 wraps. Goals: MS=80, HS=90, College=100.

DEFENSE

<u>Box Drill</u> - this is an NBA Combine drill (Lane Agility Test). Place cones in a rectangle simulating an NBA lane (16' across, 19' long).

- Start at one elbow. Sprint to baseline.
- Slide across the lane .
- Back pedal to other elbow.
- Slide across free throw line. Touch line.
- Quickly slide back to other elbow.
- Sprint to baseline.
- Slide across lane.
- Back pedal to starting line.
- Do this for time. The best time for 2020 was Jordan Bone with 9.97 seconds. Under 12 seconds for a HS player is very good.

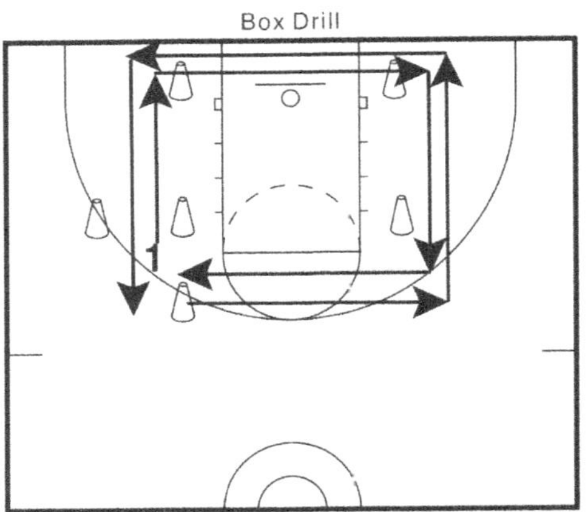

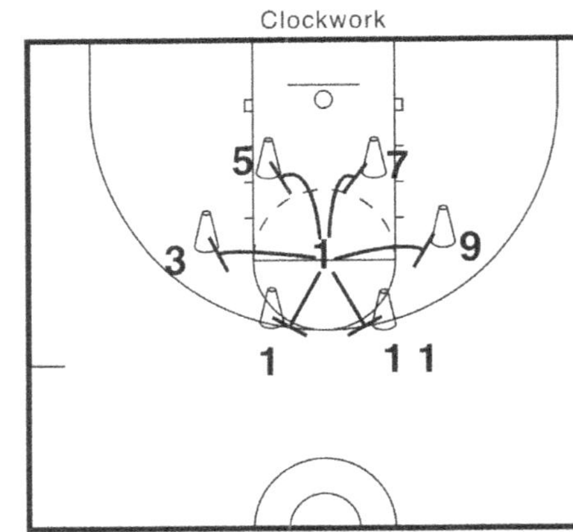

<u>Clockwork</u> - standing in the circle that surrounds the free throw line (which is 12' across), get in a defensive stance and use the proper footwork to touch certain "times" then return to the middle each time tapping feet for a 5-count. Complete the entire drill three consecutive times.

- Closeout to one o'clock angling your body toward the right sideline (taking away the middle drive).
- Shuffle to three o'clock taking away wing/gap drive.
- Drop step and sprint to five o'clock taking away baseline drive. Wall up (stand tall to contest shot or take charge).
- Drop step and sprint to seven o'clock taking away baseline drive. Wall up (stand tall to contest shot or take charge.
- Shuffle to nine o'clock taking away wing/gap drive.
- Closeout to eleven o'clock angle your body toward the left sideline (taking away the middle drive).

Full Court Zig Zag
- Sprint the length of the court (84' or 94').
- Drop step and slide back and left 3x.
- Drop step and slide back and right 3x.
- Repeat until you reach your starting point, thats one set.

In and Out Shuffle - Start in a defensive stance with hips low and back straight. Jump feet to meet in the middle and then jump them back out again. This is one repetition. Do not let your upper body bob up and down.
- 10 in and outs.
- 10 shuffles across court.
- 10 in and outs.
- 10 shuffles back to starting position. That's one set.
- Do 3 sets.

Kentucky Stomps - start in defensive stance on one side line.
- Tap for a 5-second count.

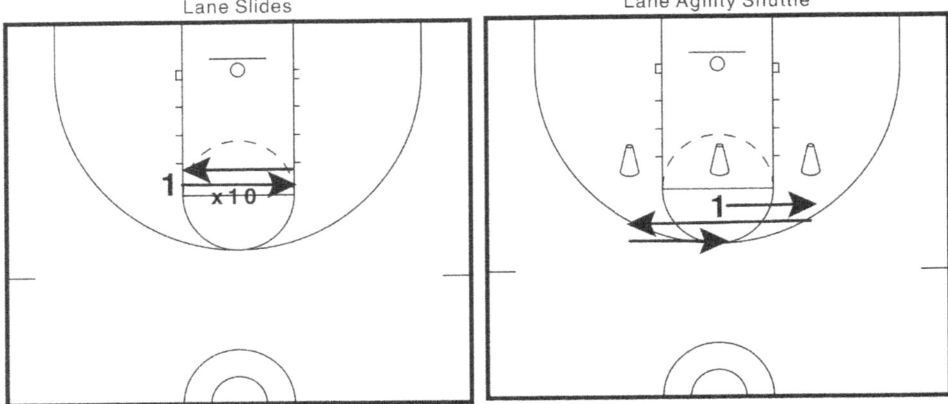

- Two explosive slides pushing with the foot on the sideline and lifting the inside foot before stomping the ground. Stomp! Stomp!
- Taps for another 5-second count.
- Do this five times or until you reach the other sideline.
- Do the same thing coming back. That's one set.
- Do three sets.

Lane Shuttle - this is an NBA combine drill. Start in the middle of the lane. The objective is to touch the outside of the lane, sprint to the other side of the lane then come back to the middle. Do this as fast as possible, anyway possible. Jordan Bone has the best time in 2020 with 2.78 seconds.

Lane Slides - slide from one side of the lane to the other = 1 touch. 10 touches as fast as possible.

Line Drills - pick a line, any line. Stay on your toes for the following routine. Keep your core tight and upper body stable. Move your feet as quickly as possible.
- Feet together side to side over the line.
- One foot in front, one foot behind line. Switch feet repeatedly.

- Criss-cross: line between your feet. Right foot up, left foot back, both land on the line. Then back out. Left foot up, Right foot back, both land on line. Then back out. Repeat.
- Do routine 3x. 1st = 15sec each, 2nd = 20sec each, 3rd = 25sec each.

<u>Perimeter Closeout</u> - SPRINT to the top of the key and closeout having hips down and hands up. Then with hands out shuffle around the perimeter down to the left baseline. Repeat and slide to right baseline. Do this 5x each side focusing on quickness.

DRIBBLE ATTACK

<u>2-Ball Series</u>
- Simultaneous 10x
- Alternating 10x
- One high, One low 10x, switch
- Windshield Wipers - same direction v-dribble 10x
- Wipers Opposites - v-dribble with balls going opposite directions 10x
- Forward and Back - on sides of body same direction 10x
- Forward and Back Opposites - opposite direction 10x
- Juggle - ball in right hand crosses over while ball in left hand is handed off to right. Continue 10x
- Zig Zag - 2 dribbles in one direction change hands and direction.
    - 1-2 Cross
    - 1-2 Thru
    - 1-2 Wrap behind back

Behind the Back Breakdown
- Crossover - jab & cross behind back under butt. 3x each
- Wrap - dribble right, wrap the ball around back without slowing down. Same thing with left. 3x each
- Delayed - 1 dribble and 2 steps in one direction before dribbling behind back. Footwork to right would be 1 dribble then left-right behind back. 3x each
- Pop - from low dribble position wrap ball around back as you hop in that direction. This is good for combo moves. 3x each

Blender Challenge - as many combo moves as possible in 1 minute. Try not to do the same combo twice in a row.

Cross-Jab Breakdown - 3x each direction
- Stationary Crossover.
- Crossover & Jab - ball moves right to left then jab right.
- Crossover, Jab and Go.

Crossover Breakdown
- Jab & Cross - jab right, sweeping cross right to left. Same thing left to right. 3x each
- Low & Tight - quick jab right, tight to body cross right to left. Same thing left to right. 3x each
- Over the Top - push the ball over would-be defender's hand. 3x each both directions
- Delayed - 2 steps in one direction before crossing over at the last second. Going right the footwork would be right-left cross. 3x each both directions

Dribble Circles
- 10 right leg low dribbles, switch direction 10 more
- 10 right leg high dribbles, switch direction 10 more

- 10 left leg low dribbles, switch direction 10 more
- 10 left leg high dribbles, switch direction 10 more
- 10 figure 8 low dribbles, switch direction 10 more
- 10 figure 8 high dribbles, switch direction 10 more
- 10 around the world low dribbles, switch direction 10 more
- 10 around the world high dribbles, switch direction 10 more

<u>In & Out Breakdown</u> - 3x each direction
- Stationary In & Out Dribble
- In & Out with Jab (of opposite foot)
- In & Out with Jab and Go

<u>In the Trench</u> - line up three cones in a row, five feet apart. Start at one cone in triple threat, dribble on right side to middle cone and perform a combo move circle around last cone and do it again. Perform same move but from the left side.
- Cross-thru
- Cross-behind
- Cross-spin
- Thru-cross
- Thru-behind
- Thru-spin
- Behind-cross
- Behind-thru
- Behind-spin

<u>Jordan Attack</u> - Double Moves or Combo Moves
- Combo Moves or Double Moves from 5 perimeter spots

- Finishing: all right-hand first attempt, all left-hand second attempt
- Goal: complete in less than 30 seconds
- Attempt at least 2 times from each side

<u>Panther Series</u>

- "2s and 3s" - fast as possible for time
  - 2 Right pound, 3 crossovers
  - 2 Left pound, 3 crossovers
  - 2 Chops (thru), 3 crossovers
  - 2 Chops (other way), 3 crossovers
  - 2 Behind Back, 3 crossovers
  - 2 Behind Back (other way), 3 crossovers
- "Ironman" - fast as possible for time. Goal = 2 min.
  - 50 Pounds (each hand)
  - 50 Crossovers
  - 50 Chops
  - 50 Behind Back
- "Burnout" - as many as possible. Goal = 200

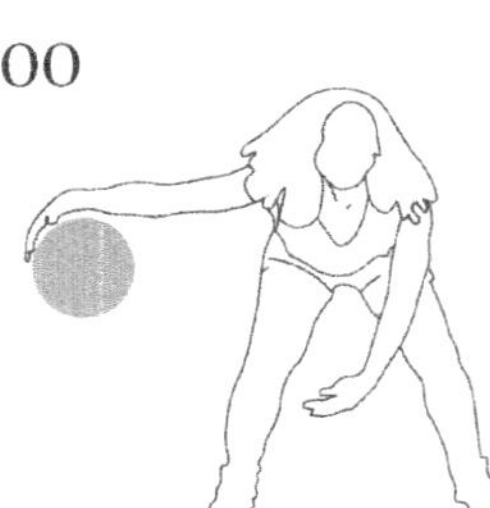

  - Right Pounds :15
  - Left Pounds :15
  - Crossovers :30
  - Chops :30
  - Behind Back :30
- "4x" - as fast as possible. Goal = 20 seconds
  - 3 crosses, 3 chops, 3 behind backs
  - 3 crosses, 3 chops, 3 behind backs
  - 3 crosses, 3 chops, 3 behind backs
  - 3 crosses, 3 chops, 3 behind backs
- "Taps" - as fast as possible
  - Tap the ball in a circle around right leg 5x, switch directions repeat

- Tap the ball in a circle around left leg 5x, switch directions repeat
- Tap the ball in a figure 8 - 5x, switch directions repeat
- Tap the ball "around your world" 5x, switch directions repeat

Spin Move Breakdown

- Magic - dribble right, step left foot across to protect the ball, switch hands and swivel head and shoulders to go left. 3x each direction
- Tight - dribble right, punch dribble and spin in one quick motion dragging the ball with right hand and releasing it after spin. Gather with left hand. 3x each direction

Thru the Legs Breakdown

- Crossover - jab & cross between legs. 3x each
- Hop - 1 dribble, hop and twist to put ball thru legs so you are now facing direction you want to go with the ball protected by your body. 3x each
- Straight Leg - 1 or 2 dribbles one direction then straight-leg plant with outside foot. Pass ball thru legs from back to front. 3x each

V-Dribble Series

- Right hand in front 10x
- Right hand on side (forward/backward) 10x
- Left hand in front 10x
- Left hand on side (forward/backward) 10x
- Sweeping crossovers 10x
- Killer-crossovers right thru to left cross 10x
- Killers-crossovers left thru to right cross 10x
- Right thru to left behind 10x

- Left thru to right behind 10x
- Crossovers behind back 10x

<u>Wing Attacks</u>
- Perform 10 single moves and 10 combos from right wing and left wing.
- Vary ways of finishing.
- Take at least 2 approach dribbles before making the move.

Finishing

<u>Interior Finishes</u> - alternate sides of the rim on every attempt.
- Mikans - 10 makes
- Reverse Mikans - 10 makes
- Drop Steps Baseline - 10 makes
- Drop Steps Middle Jump Hooks - 10 makes
- Rebound and Power Dribble Opposite - 10 makes

<u>Lillard Layups</u> - Set up 3 consecutive cones about 5 feet apart from foul line to 3 pt line to 5' out. Make a move on each cone and make a layup. 3 makes on right side then 3 on left side before moving on.
- In and Out dribble to outside hand layup
- Drop and Go (hesitation) to inside hand layup
- Combo move to 2-foot layup

<u>Level One Finishing Series</u> - start on wing, drive and finish and continue to other wing for the same move.
- One foot outside hand
- Two feet outside hand
- Middle drive, finish opposite with outside hand
- Baseline drive, reverse finish

- Floater

<u>Level Two Finishing Series</u>

- Euro step
- Middle drive, opposite finish with inside hand
- Rondo (fake above move, pivot and jump hook)
- Pro-hop (punch dribble, jump stop, switch hands)
- Stride stop, step thru finish with opposite hand

<u>Level Three Finishing Series</u>

- Two feet absorb contact and extend outside arm
- Bump and Body - two feet go through contact
- Up and Under Outside Hand - jump off two feet on one side of the rim, switch hands and finish on other side of the rim.
- Up and Under Inside Hand - jump off two feet on one side of the rim, twist body to finish with the same hand on other side of the rim.
- Switch Hands - jump of one foot with ball in outside hand, switch hands and finish on opposite side.

<u>Mount Zion</u> - "Interior Finishes" routine. Every shot is worth 2 points. Maximum = 50 pts.

Shooting

50 in 3 - Shoot 10 three pointers from 5 spots in 3 minutes. Best to have two basketballs, a rebounder and a passer. But one rebounder who wants to hustle will do.

<u>Arc Shooting</u> - 10 shots as you move around in an arc after each shot. 3', 6', 10', 15', 20'. (50 total shots)

<u>Can't Miss Two</u> - how many jumpshots (or 3s) can you make without missing 2 in a row?

<u>Elevator Shooting</u> - start 10' from the rim. After a make, move back to 15' and again to 20'. You can't move to the next shot until you make it from the previous distance. Do this from both baselines, both wings and the middle. To add difficulty force yourself to make all 3 in a row before moving on. (If you miss the 3 pointer you must go back to the 10' shot.) 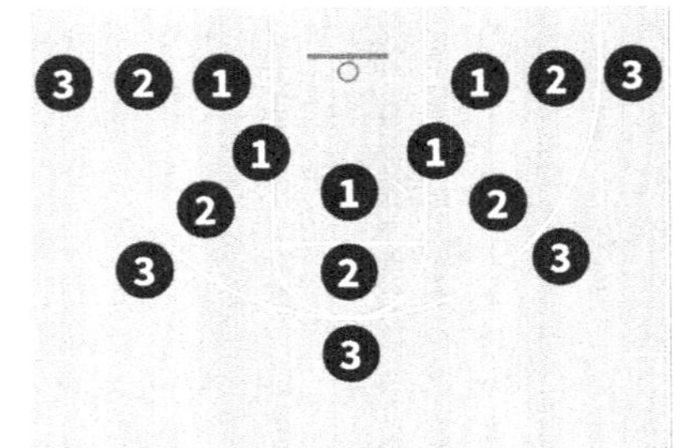

<u>Free Throws in a Row</u> - how many free throws can you make without missing?

<u>Holy Cross</u> - You have 1 minute to take and make as many three-pointers as possible. You must get your own rebound.

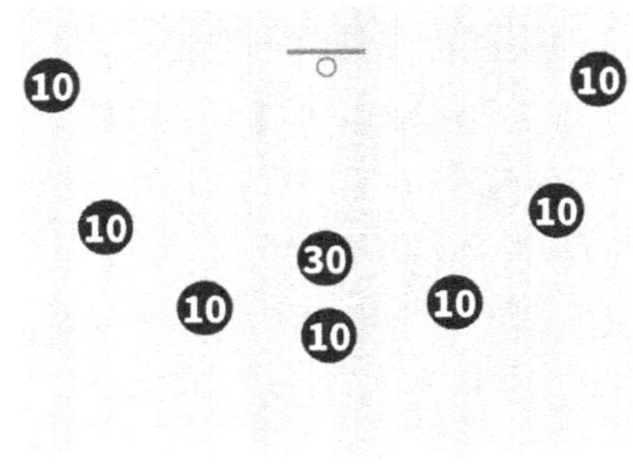

<u>Loaded Cannon</u> - A total of 100 makes.
- 10 threes from each corner
- 10 threes from each wing
- 10 threes from each slot
- 10 threes from the top of the key
- 30 free throws

Make 3 - Make a jump-shot, right dribble pull-up jumper, left dribble pull jumper from 5 spots on the court. Both baselines, both wings, top of the key. 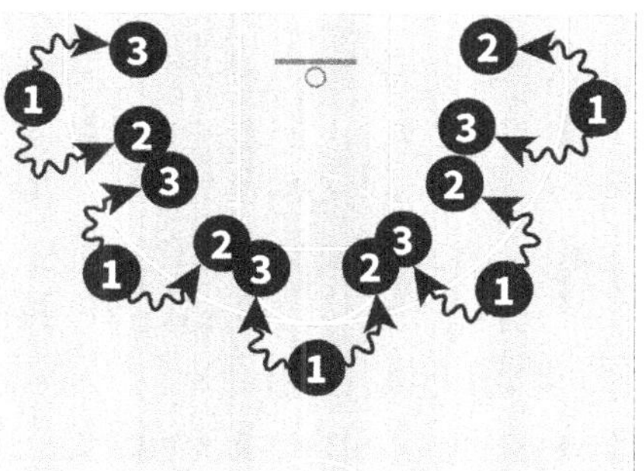

Midrange Challenge - 15-18 foot jumpers from 5 different spots. Make 10 from each. Both baselines, both wings, middle.

NBA Shooting - from 5 spots (corners, wings, top of the key) you will go through the following routine:

- Make as many 3-pointers as you can without missing (3 pts each)
- After miss, make as many midrange jumpers as possible (2 pts each)
- After miss, shoot 1 layup (1pt) and move to the next spot
- You don't move to the next shot until you miss, except you only shoot 1 layup.
- Goal for a college player is 100 points

<u>Sixes</u> - Move from baseline to elbow shooting midrange jumpers until you make 6. Then move elbow to elbow - make 6. Then move elbow to baseline on the other side of court - make 6. Finish with 2 free throws. Goal = 2 minutes. 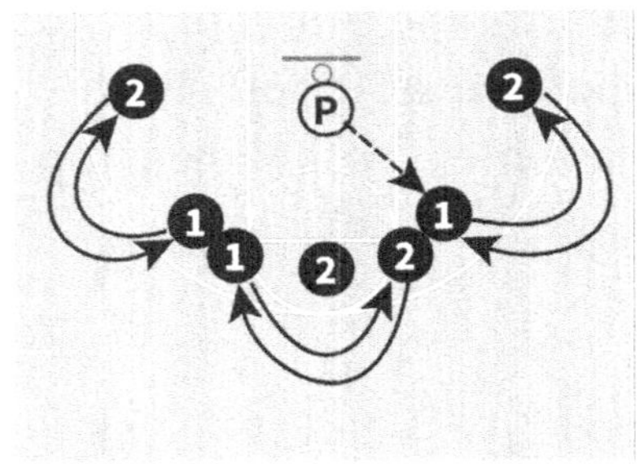

<u>Sixes Off the Dribble</u> - Catch on the wing and dribble to baseline for a jumper. Go back to the wing. Now dribble to elbow for a jumper. Continue until you make 6, then move to the top of the key. Alternate dribbling to each elbow for jumpers until 6 makes. Then move to the other wing and alternate dribbling to elbow and baseline until you make 6 jumpers. Finish with 2 free throws. Goal = 3 minutes.

<u>Weber State License to Shoot</u> - Try to make 30 three-pointers out of 50 tries. Do this 5 times for your "License to Shoot." The drill begins when you make your first shot

- 10 spot-up threes from corner, wing, top, wing, corner and back around (2 from each)
- 10 pin-down threes - touch the paint between each shot as if you were running off a down screen
- 10 transition threes - touch half court between each shot and run to the wing. 5 from right and 5 from left. Passer is in near circle at half court.
- 10 trailer threes - touch half court between each shot and run down the middle for a three at the top of the key. 5 passes from right wing, 5 from left wing.
- 10 Spot-up threes just like you started

Footwork

<u>Jab Series</u> - catch in triple threat position
- Jumper
- Jab & Jumper
- Jab & Go same side for layup
- Jab & Rip opposite for layup
- Jab & Go for pull-up jumper
- Jab & Rip for pull-up jumper
- Jab & Go for side-step jumper
- Jab & Rip for step-back jumper

<u>100 pt Challenge</u> - the above routine from 5 spots on the court (each baseline, each wing, top of the key). 1st 2 shots and last 2 shots are worth 3 pts each, middle 4 are worth 2pts each. Opportunity for 20 points at each spot.

<u>Squaring Up Series</u> - standing at the baseline toss the ball to the elbow with backspin so it comes back to you. Catch facing half court and square up to the basket for a jumpshot. Alternate side to side until you make 10.
- Right foot front pivot
- Left foot front pivot
- Right foot reverse pivot
- Left foot reverse pivot

<u>Steve Alford Challenge</u> - Utilizing one of the techniques from the "squaring up" series (front pivot, reverse pivot), give yourself 1 point for a make and -2 points for a miss. If you get to +10 you win, -10 you lose.

<u>Post Moves Series</u> - alternating from block to block, spin the ball to yourself and perform the following moves
- Pivot baseline and finish. 10x.
- Pivot baseline & step thru. 10x.
- Drop step with power dribble. 10x.
- Dribble middle and jump stop. 10x.
- Dribble middle and drop step opposite. 10x

<u>Offensive Rebounding Series</u> Grab the ball and score 3 ways: finish, finish opposite side, tip in. Always rebound with two hands (John Calipari rule).
- Throw the ball high into the air so it bounces up near the rim. Jump as high as you can and snatch it.
- Throw the ball off the backboard, jump as high as you can and snatch it.
- Throw the ball off the backboard from one side of the lane so it lands on the other side of the lane. Run and jump to snatch the ball out of the air.

<u>Board Man Gets Paid Challenge</u> - Perform the offensive rebounding series and keep score. Every attempt is worth 1 point. A rebound and finish = 1pt. Any mistake (missed layup, bobbled rebound) = 0 pts.

<u>Next Level Jab Series</u> - "Show" means swing the ball in front of the defender. "Punch" refers to a pound dribble meant to enable steps without traveling.
- Show-Punch Jumper - Swing ball to strong hand and punch dribble to make defender retreat.
- Show-Punch Hesi-Jumper - add hesitation before shooting.
- Show-Cross Jumper - swing ball but cross it over using a flick of the wrist.

- Show-Cross Hesi-Jumper
- Show-Behind Jumper
- Show-Behind Hesi-Jumper
- Step Across Punch Spin - step across so your back is facing the defender, punch dribble and immediately spin back to strong side.
- Step Across Punch Go - step across, punch dribble, fake spin and drive weakside.
- Step Across Lean & Roll - step across, lean on defender, as soon as you feel resistance roll/spin into drive.
- Step Across Back Down & Roll

<u>On the Move Series</u>
- Pin Downs - pass to a teammate and run toward them to catch the ball.
    - Pop - set up defender and come off screen for straight cut to open space
    - Curl - as if defender is chasing you, curl around screen for close finish
    - Fade - as if defender went under the screen fade away from screener
- Flares - pass to a teammate and run away from them to open space to catch the ball 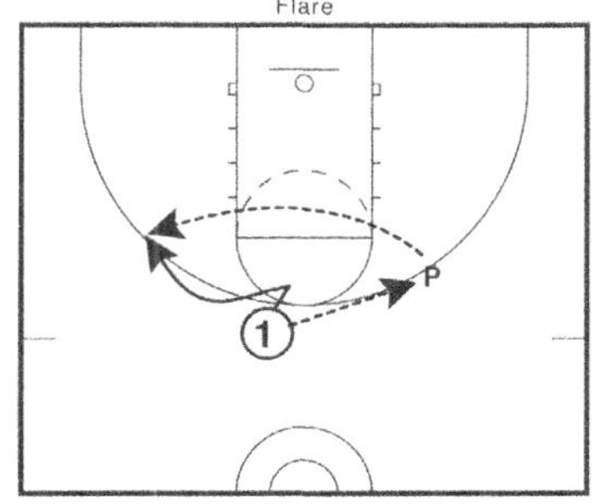
    - Flare - Pass and fade away from passer.
    - Pick and Pop - set ball screen then fade away to open space.
    - Ghost Screen - fake a ball screen and fade to open space.

<u>Pop-Curl-Fade Challenge</u> - Every shot is worth 2 points for a max of 36 points. Take one of each of the following shots on one side of the court and then repeat the routine on the other side.

- Pop - run straight out to the perimeter.
  - Catch and shoot
  - Catch and go pull-up
  - Catch and rip pull-up
- Curl - run around screen for an interior shot.
  - Layup
  - Layup opposite
  - Floater
- Fade - fake curl and back pedal to the corner.
  - Catch and shoot
  - Catch and go side-step
  - Catch and rip step-back

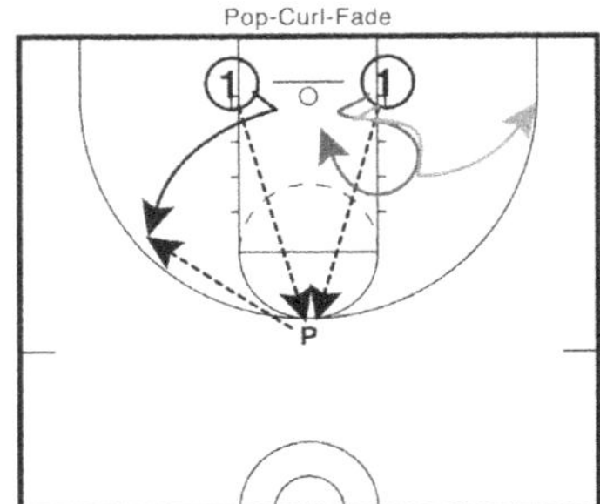

References

1. Krzyzewski, Mike with Jamie K. Spatola, *The Gold Standard: Building a World-Class Team* (Business Plus, 2010).

2. Guest, Edgar Albert, "Defeat", https://www.poeticous.com/edgar-albert-guest/defeat-no-one-is-beat-till-he-quits

3. Love, Dave, "The Art of Shooting with NBA Shooting Instructor Dave Love," *The Jim Huber Show.* Podcast Audio. (November 17, 2016). https://www.breakthroughbasketball.com/podcast/31/

4. Gervais, Michael, *Finding Master Podcast* (November 20, 2015).

5. Frederick, David, *Problems of Democracy Lecture* (2001).

6. Kerr, James, *Legacy: What the All Blacks Can Teach Us About the Business of Life* (Constable 2015).

7. Divine, Mark, *The Way of the Seal: Think Like an Elite Warrior to Lead and Succeed* (Reader's Digest 2018).

8. Sinek, Simon, *Start With Why: How Great Leaders Inspire Everyone to Take Action* (Portfolia 2011).

9. Pete Carroll, "Pete Carroll: Competing to Be Your Best," *Finding Mastery Podcast,* Podcast Audio. (April 27, 2016).

10. Thayer, L. E., "Growth"

11. Wooden, John, *Pyramid of Success*

12. Wooden, John, *Wooden: A Lifetime of Observations and Reflections* (McGraw-Hill, 1997).

13. Grover, Tim, *Jump Attack: The Formula for Explosive Athletic Performance,* (Simon & Schuster, 2014)

14. Wintle, Walter D., "Thinking"

15. Wooden, John, "Tomorrow"

16. Beck, John, "Weight Room Myths"

17. Councillor, *Mastery of Life,* "Always a Way" p 193 (Continental Book Company, 1924)

18. Dumas, John Lee, *Entrepreneur on Fire.* Podcast Audio

Made in the USA
Coppell, TX
13 December 2020